Further Praise for *The Morning They Came for Us*

"Devastating.... Like the work of the Belarussian Nobel laureate Svetlana Alexievich, Ms. di Giovanni's book gives voice to ordinary people living through a dark time in history; and like Anthony Shadid's powerful 2005 book, *Night Draws Near* (which recounted the aftermath of the American invasion of Iraq), it chronicles the intimate fallout that war has on women, children and families. A longtime reporter who covered the wars in Bosnia, Chechnya and Sierra Leone, Ms. di Giovanni writes here with urgency and anguish—determined to testify to what she has witnessed because she wants 'people never to forget.' ... Her testimony is contained here in this searing and necessary book." —Michiko Kakutani, *New York Times*

"Necessary, difficult and elating. [Di Giovanni's] reporting from the Syrian revolution and war is clear-eyed and engaged in the best sense—engaged in the human realm rather than the abstractly political. . . . Such reporters as Giovanni, who not only visit but also live (and often die) through wars not their own, are heroic. These are the Marie Colvins, Paul Conroys, Ali Mustafas of journalism, reporters motivated by commitment to the act of witnessing." —Robin Yassin-Kassab, *Guardian*

"It is crucial to reveal the human stories behind the news—and in *The Morning They Came for Us*, Janine di Giovanni does this with heartbreaking eloquence.... Her account of Syria is a testimony to the power of empathy, conscience and understanding." —Elif Shafak, *Financial Times*

"*The Morning They Came for Us* moves from a cosmopolitan 'bubble of parties' in 2011 to 'the aftermath of a barrel bomb' today as di Giovanni observes slaughter and rape with the equal (if occasionally opposing and heartbreaking) empathies of war correspondent and mother."   —Lea Carpenter, *Vanity Fair*

"Not every journalist can break through and reach readers in a deeper place. It requires courage to bear witness to the horrors of war, and also the ability to narrate the experience in an impactive way. The writer needs to be able to not just tell, but show how a country falls apart, how people lose their beloved ones, and how friends and neighbors turn into enemies.... [Di Giovanni] does exactly this.... [A] must read filled with bitter realities. It is a call to the outside world not to forget what is happening in Syria."
     —Denise Hassanzade Ajiri, *Christian Science Monitor*

"What life is like for ordinary Syrians who have stayed behind is the subject of Janine di Giovanni's heartbreaking book.... [U]nsensational but unsparing.... [I]t is individual stories, rather than victims counted in the millions, that reveal the terrible cost of leaving dictators in place for the sake of 'stability.'"   —Joan Smith, *Observer*

"Di Giovanni writes vividly and we see with her how Damascene supporters of Assad drift away as the brutality of his rule became impossible to deny.... Di Giovanni explains to us how horrible it all really is."   —Sam Kiley, *Evening Standard*

"Elegant dispatches ... offer a snapshot of the time when naive hopes spiraled into nightmare.... Di Giovanni, who covered the Balkan conflict with distinction, does not hide emotions as she explores the use of rape in war once again and her stories, such as that of a shattered young woman detained after publicising protests on social media, are deeply disturbing."

—Ian Birrell, *Spectator*

"Di Giovanni presents a devastating picture of the horrors of civil war and the disintegration of Syrian society."

—Elizabeth Hayford, *Library Journal*

"[Di Giovanni] is a master of war reporting, especially its civilian side. Thanks to her bitter sacrifice, Western readers may begin to appreciate the chaos that Syrian refugees continue to flee. This brilliant, necessary book will hopefully do for Syria what Herr's *Dispatches* (1977) did for Vietnam."

—*Kirkus Reviews*, starred review

"With a potent mix of sensitivity and outrage, di Giovanni relates firsthand accounts of deprivation and suffering from the people caught up in the conflict.... [T]heir stories reveal in harrowing detail the horrific nature of the war. The expert perspective of this seasoned war correspondent proves invaluable to understanding Syria today."   —Bridget Thoreson, *Booklist*, starred review

"[Di Giovanni's] work, informed by her extensive experience as a journalist, shows a keen ability to capture violent conflicts from multiple sides.... This book, haunted by the international failure to intervene effectively, gives readers an on-the-ground experience of the devastating seasons that followed the promise of the Arab Spring.... [Di Giovanni] makes its reality fully tangible and tragic."   —*Publishers Weekly*, starred review

BY THE SAME AUTHOR

Eve Arnold: Magnum Legacy
Ghosts by Daylight: A Memoir of War and Love
The Place at the End of the World: Essays from the Edge
Madness Visible: A Memoir of War
The Quick and the Dead: Under Siege in Sarajevo
Against the Stranger: Lives in Occupied Territory

THE MORNING
THEY CAME FOR US

Dispatches from Syria

Janine di Giovanni

LIVERIGHT PUBLISHING CORPORATION
A Division of W. W. Norton & Company
Independent Publishers Since 1923
New York · London

In memory of my beloved brother, Joseph, who died
suddenly on 11 August 2015

Copyright © 2016 by Janine di Giovanni
First American Edition 2016
First published as a Liveright paperback 2017

Maps by John Gilkes

For information about permission to reproduce selections from this book,
write to Permissions, Liveright Publishing Corporation, a division of
W. W. Norton & Company, Inc., 500 Fifth Avenue, New York, NY 10110

For information about special discounts for bulk purchases, please contact
W. W. Norton Special Sales at specialsales@wwnorton.com or 800-233-4830

Manufacturing by Quad Graphics, Fairfield
Production manager: Anna Oler

Library of Congress Cataloging-in-Publication Data

Names: Di Giovanni, Janine, date. author.
Title: The morning they came for us : dispatches from Syria /
Janine di Giovanni.
Description: New York : Liveright Publishing Corporation, [2016] |
Includes bibliographical references and index.
Identifiers: LCCN 2016007537 | ISBN 9780871407139 (hardcover)
Subjects: LCSH: Syria—History—Civil War, 2011—Personal narratives, Syrian.
Classification: LCC DS98.6 .D54 2016 | DDC 956.9104/2—dc23
LC record available at http://lccn.loc.gov/2016007537

ISBN: 978-1-63149-295-2 pbk.

Liveright Publishing Corporation
500 Fifth Avenue, New York, N.Y. 10110
www.wwnorton.com

W. W. Norton & Company Ltd.
15 Carlisle Street, London W1D 3BS

1 2 3 4 5 6 7 8 9 0

'Only the dead know the end of war.'

Plato

'In such a world of conflict, a world of victims and executioners, it is the job of thinking people . . . not to be on the side of the executioners.'

Howard Zinn, *A People's History of the United States*

'Wars have no memory, and nobody has the courage to understand them until there are no voices left to tell what happened, until the moment comes when we no longer recognize them and they return, with another face and another name, to devour what they left behind.'

Carlos Ruiz Zafón, *The Shadow of the Wind*

Contents

Maps   x

Introduction   xiii

1 Damascus – Thursday 28 June 2012   1

2 Latakia – Thursday 14 June 2012   11

3 Ma'loula and Damascus – June–November 2012   37

4 Homs – Thursday 8 March 2012   60

5 Darayya – Saturday 25 August 2012   74

6 Zabadani – Saturday 8 September 2012   89

7 Homs, Bab al-Sebaa Street – Sunday
   14 October 2012   104

8 Aleppo – Sunday 16 December 2012   120

Epilogue – November 2016   160

Notes   174

Acknowledgements   178

Chronology   183

Index   201

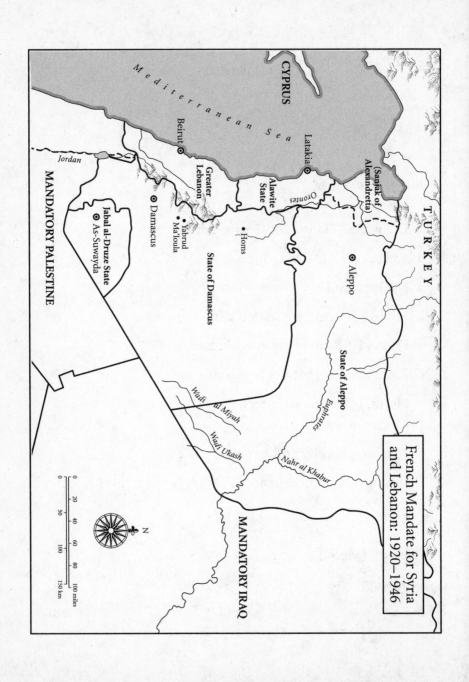

French Mandate for Syria and Lebanon: 1920–1946

MANDATORY PALESTINE

MANDATORY IRAQ

TURKEY

CYPRUS

Mediterranean Sea

Beirut

Latakia

(Sanjak of Alexandretta)

Jordan

Greater Lebanon

Alawite State

Orontes

Damascus

Yabrud

Ma'loula

Homs

Aleppo

State of Damascus

State of Aleppo

Jabal al-Druze State

As-Suwayda

Wadi al Miyah

Wadi Ukash

Euphrates

Nahr al Khabur

N

0   20   40   60   80   100 miles

0   50   100   150 km

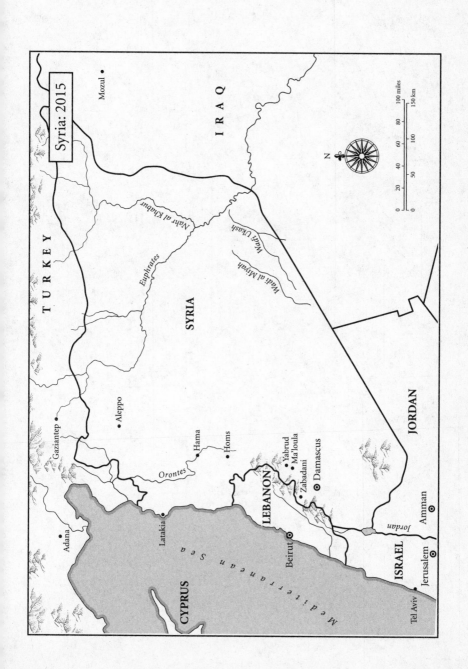

Syria: 2015

TURKEY

IRAQ

Mozul

Nahr al Khabur

Euphrates

Wadi al Miyah

Wadi Ukash

SYRIA

Gaziantep

Aleppo

Adana

Hama

Homs

Orontes

Latakia

LEBANON

Yabrud
Ma'loula
Zabadani   ◉ Damascus

Beirut ◎

CYPRUS

Mediterranean Sea

JORDAN

Jordan

Amman ◎

ISRAEL

Tel Aviv
Jerusalem ◎

N

0   20   40   60   80   100 miles
0   50   100   150 km

Introduction

It was the winter of 2011, and I was in Belgrade. The war that had destroyed Yugoslavia had been over for many years, but I was working on a project tracing war criminals. It was an intractable task, but the potent emotion I felt towards the Balkan wars and their aftermath was not rational.

It was a terrible fever – not unlike malaria, recurring in your bloodstream for ever once you got it – that had gripped me since I had reported from Bosnia in the early 1990s. The men who had caused such evil and such harm, who had burnt villages and bombed schools and hospitals, who had mutilated children and raped women en masse, were still living in villages, going fishing at weekends and having picnics with their grandchildren. It made me feel physically ill thinking about them living unreservedly while their victims were dead; and I would trail the events that led to the downfall of that sorrowful country. In Sarajevo one year, I spent days, which turned into weeks, with the man who ran the morgue during the war. He had not only arranged the bodies and prepared them for burial but he also diligently kept notebooks with every name, every detail of their time and their cause of death (bullets, shrapnel, explosion). He called it *The Book of the Dead*. One morning, he arrived at the morgue and found his only son, a young front-line soldier, laid out on the slab.

He survived and grew old, and when I found him two decades after the war ended, we went through the books carefully. But his partner at the morgue, a less robust man, had killed himself years before.

I wanted my fever to break, but it never did. Throughout the new millennium, criminals from the Balkan wars, rapists and murderers, went unpunished. I talked to women who had been kept in camps and violated sometimes a dozen times a day; women who were forced to carry their rapists' children. Yet post-war, owing to the division of the country, and the fact that no one really knew who their neighbours were any more, these women had to face their rapists daily, passing them in the local shops or on the street, at the schools where they took their children. It was the victims, not the perpetrators, who dropped their eyes in shame when they passed one another.

But some of them met their fate. Radovan Karadzic, the psychiatrist, football fanatic, poet and leader of the Bosnian Serbs, who led the puppet regime for Slobodan Milosevic, the former president of Serbia, had been caught while riding on a bus in 2008. He had been in disguise, and had been in hiding since the war ended in 1995, living under a false name and posing as a New Age healer. Karadzic is, at this time of writing, being tried for alleged war crimes but no verdict has been reached.

Slobodan Milosevic, the leader of Serbia throughout these wars, had been carted off to The Hague in his bedroom slippers by helicopter in 2001. The day it happened I was also in Belgrade, but I drove all night to get to Sarajevo, the city he had hated and almost destroyed, to witness the reaction of the people. I expected to find jubilation that Milosevic was getting his just deserts, but instead I found weariness. My friends – former soldiers, lawyers, students, doctors, mothers, teachers – were too tired to celebrate, to think that this meant something in terms of retribution. Everyone just wanted to forget about the war that had devoured them alive.

I felt the greatest revenge was that the man who had caused such pain to his own people would sit in a jail cell in The Hague for the rest of his life, but Milosevic did not, in fact, face justice. He was found dead in his cell in 2006, under mysterious circumstances. Some said suicide; some said his devoted followers had slipped him a pill which made his heart quicken and burst; some say he died of heartbreak. The fact was, this wicked man had died before justice had been served.

Still at large on that winter afternoon in January 2011, while I sat in a freezing café in New Belgrade talking to men who had once fought alongside him, was Ratko Mladic, the general who had led his men on a rampage and who had headed the assault on Srebrenica. He was sleeping soundly in some village in Serbia, protected by his followers, while the families of the 8,000 men and boys killed in Srebrenica had to live with their ghosts, their memories of their loved ones fading more and more into the distance every day. At the moment, he stands accused of war crimes – no verdict has been reached as the trial has not yet concluded.

I was not a criminal investigator, and I knew that I would not be the one to march up to Mladic and put the hand-cuffs on him before he was arrested, but in some ways, I had much more freedom than police. I could sit in cafés where

Mladic's followers gathered to drink their morning tea, and ask where he had last been seen. I could sit by the grave of his daughter, who had tragically killed herself during the war, and ask the woman who kept the graves when she had last seen him; what his mood was; how he appeared physically. I could try to put myself in his mindset. In building up a portrait of the tormented Mladic, I wanted also to make him immortal: as immortal as those it is claimed he had murdered (though he denies murder).

In short, I wanted people never to forget.

While I was in the middle of compiling notes of interviews with his old school friends, his soldiers, his cadres and his loyalists, the Arab Spring began – first the Jasmine Revolution in Tunisia, then Egypt. I was watching Tahrir Square in full meltdown on television, flicking from station to station, the images of the crowds growing larger and larger, and waiting out the countdown for the end of the reign of Hosni Mubarak. I had started my working life in the Middle East as a young postgraduate student two decades earlier, and it had drawn me in, by the heart and the guts, as much as Bosnia had.

I finished my work and by the time Mladic was caught, in May 2011, I was in Tunisia, then Egypt, Libya, Iraq, and finally Syria. It seemed I could transfer my obsession from the Balkans to Syria, which was the last in the chain, in the string of pearls of the revolutions. Syria began as a peaceful one, but, as I write this four years in, the revolution has since spiralled into a gruesome, a brutal, a seemingly forever war.

As I roamed across the country, moving from one side to the other, sometimes legally (with a Syrian regime visa

stamped in my passport) and sometimes illegally (crossing various borders to reach rebel sides of Syria), I tried
not to draw comparisons with Bosnia. But it was difficult
not to do so. There were the same floods of refugees, the
same burnt-out villages, and the same women driven out in
terror, because paramilitaries were on the march and they
feared being raped. After all the lessons we had learnt from
the brutality of the wars in the 1990s – Rwanda, Somalia,
Liberia, Sierra Leone, Chechnya – we were allowing it to
happen again.

A friend, LR, a diplomat who had shared with me many
experiences of post-war Bosnia and the lessons that had not
been learnt, who told me once not to take a job in a certain
part of the world, 'because you will be angry all the time and
it is an anger that you will never be able to reconcile', warned
me not to start working in Syria. He said it would engulf me
as Bosnia had done, and he suggested gently that this was
probably not a good thing emotionally.

Even so, I went.

I

Damascus – Thursday 28 June 2012

On an early morning in May 2012, one year into the Syrian revolution, I made my first trip to Damascus. It was a suffocating, early summer day with a hazy, opaque light. I arrived from Beirut in a local taxi, which I had hired for slightly less than 100 dollars, paid in cash. The driver picked me up on the road to Damascus and made a joke about St Paul's Damascene conversion, as he loaded my bags into the boot of the car. Then we drove into another country, leaving behind Beirut with its modern beach clubs and crowded Thursday hairdressers and balmy restaurants and noisy clubs, and drove to another land, one that was teetering on the edge of war.

In the New Testament, it says that St Paul was on this same road sometime in the first century AD, when an event occurred. I am not sure, and neither are historians or religious fanatics, whether he heard a voice or was given a sign from God, or whether he just had a sharp and painful understanding that his life was not on the right track. At any rate, a mystic conversion occurred. Paul ceased persecuting the early Christians and instead became a loyal follower of Jesus. His life changed for ever.

It does not take long to get to Syria from Lebanon, which gives an idea of how brutally the land was torn up and fashioned into artificial countries after the First World War, once the Ottoman Empire had collapsed. The modern Syrian state was established as a French mandate, after many false promises, lies and deceptions of the Arabs by the French and British. It left the Syrians (particularly the Alawites, who had felt most oppressed by French rule) with a wilful desire for self-determination. Syria finally gained independence in April 1946, as a parliamentary republic. What followed next was a series of coups, until the Arab Republic of Syria was established in 1963 in a Ba'athist coup d'état planned and led by several men, including Hafez Assad, father of the current president, Bashar.

Looking at that timeline of betrayal and violence, the groundwork had already been laid for the tragedy that would evolve decades after those maps had been redrawn by colonial interlocutors. It seemed forcefully inevitable.

The first thing I saw once I crossed the border into the Syrian hinterland was an enormous colour portrait of Bashar al-Assad, his already vivid eyes tinted blue to make their colour even more intense. The second thing I noticed was a Dunkin' Donuts, which seemed odd, even in a sophisticated country like Syria. It was an awkward juxtaposition, so blatant a symbol of Western commercialism – not a small café serving coffee but a sugar-infested paradise – on a highway leading to Damascus.

As it turned out, the Dunkin' Donuts was not what I suspected. Although it looked like the solidly American version, down to the branded signs and decoration, it only sold toasted cheese sandwiches. I bought one, and was watched all the while as three mustachioed men smoking cigarettes – obviously Mukhabarat, secret police – stood around the bar, while one of them toasted it. My driver was waiting, twitchy and nervous, and hustled me out once the sandwich had been served.

The atmosphere in Damascus was equally paranoid, something like the old days in Iraq under Saddam Hussein. There was an unspoken quality, a silence despite the blaring horns of those caught in traffic. People whispered when out in public. When a waiter arrived at a table, the people at that table stopped talking. The Mukhabarat could easily have been the same men who had followed me in Iraq a decade before – those same cheap leather jackets, the same badly trimmed, downward-turned moustaches. Many of the Ba'athists I knew from Saddam's portfolio had, in fact, run to another country of Ba'athists after he was killed – to Syria.

I had come to Syria because I wanted to see a country before it tumbled down the rabbit-hole of war. During that first trip, in May 2012, Syria was just on the brink. You could be exacting about definitions and call it an armed conflict between two factions (later three, then four, then more), but I had seen war start like this before, and it was descending on Syria with stunning velocity. The world stood by watching.

I had a visa, therefore I was there legally, but anyway, I felt uneasy: I was watched, observed and followed. I checked into a hotel, the Dama Rose, where the United Nations monitors were also staying: morose men who were no longer allowed to operate because they had been attacked too often. They sat drinking coffee after coffee and making jokes about the bar downstairs, which was usually frequented by lithe young Russian girls whom they called 'Natashas'. In a few weeks' time, even the Natashas would flee, even though Putin being Assad's ally had made it easy for them to get visas to enter the country.

One Thursday – the day that is the start of the Muslim weekend – I returned to the hotel after a day of talking to people who were uncertain whether or not their country would exist in a year or two. They were Christians, but liberal. They did not support the government's crushing of peaceful rebellions, but nor did they support an armed resistance. At that point, I was trying to describe the various supporters and detractors of Assad. There were rebels who were fighting him; there were activists who were launching a digital war, using Facebook, YouTube and Twitter as ammunition; and then there were those who had protested in places like Homs in the beginning but had dropped out altogether when some of their fellow activists took up arms.

In a café in Paris, on a bitterly cold day earlier that year, I had met with Fadwa Suleiman, a graceful Alawite actress who, in the very beginning of the revolution, led the protests and became something of a celebrity (before that she had starred in Syrian soaps). Because she was an Alawite, the same ethnic group as Assad, and a protester calling for freedom from the regime, she was instantly branded as the face of the revolution. But she said things had changed. She was saddened to see that 'the revolution is not going in the right direction, that it is becoming armed, that the opposition which wanted to resist peacefully is playing the game of the regime, and that the country is heading for sectarian war.' 'I didn't want to leave Syria,' she added, 'but I didn't have the choice. I was being threatened and I was becoming a threat for the activists who were helping me.'

Then there were what I called 'the Believers', Assad's followers, some of them as devoted to him as St Paul had been to Jesus, but others who were simply concerned that, as a minority of a minority – Alawites are an offshoot of the Shia branch of Islam – they would disappear if the radical Sunnis came to power.

There was a sub-faction of the Believers who only wanted to save their own skin: they did not want to get hauled away to jail by Assad. They privately did not approve of the regime's torture cells and bombing raids on Aleppo, but they found the news hard to believe, and, above all, they did not want the radical Islamists in power.

Then there was another category: those who believed in nothing other than staying alive, putting a meal on the table, stepping across a street without getting sprayed with shrapnel, or travelling in a car without getting stuck in traffic next to a car bomber.

Sometimes the categories shifted. The longer I stayed, the wider became the range of activists I would come across. I knew some who became Believers after ISIS – the Islamic State of Iraq and Syria, sometimes called ISIL, sometimes called Daesh in Arabic – came to power, simply because they did not want to live under that kind of Islam: one where women doctors were beheaded, where children were taught to hate anyone who was not like them, where only the most literal, most radical form of Islam was accepted. There were also rebels who shifted sides, moving from being supporters of the Free Syrian Army to part of Jabhat al-Nusra (the al-Qaeda faction in Syria), and then making the leap to ISIS.

Equally, many Believers were also losing faith. The Foreign Ministry spokesman that spring and summer was Jihad Makdissi, a Christian with a Muslim name and a degree from the Sorbonne in Paris. In his office at the Ministry, Jihad explained how his country was a 'melting pot' of ethnicity: Greek Orthodox, Christians, Sunni Kurds, Shias, Alawites and Jews. He was rational, intelligent and thoughtful, and it was obvious why he was put in that position – to give a gentler face to the regime.

But Jihad did not stay much longer. One year after my first visit to Syria, I would open the paper and see that Makdissi had defected with his wife and children to the Gulf, making him for ever *persona non grata* – at least under the Assad regime. Some time after that, I met him for lunch in a businessmen's café in Geneva, a few days before the failed Geneva II talks. Makdissi, who was leaning towards a political career, but was not entirely clear about what his platform would be, told me about his final days in Syria: 'I realized that things I had accepted before, I would no longer be able to accept.'

Suleiman, the actress, also fled from Homs to Damascus, thence to Jordan, and finally to France. She said it was in Homs that she saw Sunnis who had initially carried weapons only to defend themselves begin to use these arms to attack regime forces. 'It was then that I understood,' she said, acknowledging that what she had thought would be a peaceful uprising was turning into war. She blamed, above all, not the Syrians themselves, but the 'other countries' (Saudi, Qatar, Kuwait) that were 'arming the Syrian streets. . . Those people are willing to do anything to take power in the same way that Bashar al-Assad is ready to do anything to stay in power.'

Fadwa wasn't that happy in Paris, she said; she missed her friends, her family and her old life. The life of someone in exile is always hard, more so when your country is in the midst of war and you are outside it, watching through a frosted-glass window. The actress had cut off her long hair when she started marching in Homs, as a symbolic gesture of protest, and in the Paris café that afternoon, with her short hair and big sweater, she looked scrawny, abandoned and cold. But she wasn't going back, she said, running her fingers through the hair she had willingly and somehow symbolically cut off, until Syria was a country she once again could recognize.

The pool party at my hotel that Thursday in early summer 2012 seemed to betoken the last days of a spoilt empire that was about to implode. Smoke was rising in the background from shelling in the southern suburbs, and a gaunt Russian Natasha was dancing clumsily near the pool, oblivious to the explosions. Syrian women with complicated hairstyles involving hairpieces and extensions, blow-dryings and coloured gels, paraded in full makeup, bikinis and high heels. The men wore Vilebrequin-style swimming trunks and drank Lebanese beer with a lime down the neck of a bottle and a salt-rimmed glass. A remix version of Adele's 'Someone Like You' thumped from a stage.

I stood on my balcony and watched the smoke from the bombing in the suburbs, but I also looked at the bacchanalian scene below – at the denial of the beginnings of the drum roll of war. One by one by one, these people's lives were

7

falling apart, and before they knew it each and every one of them would be betrayed. But the bubble had not yet burst.

For several weeks running, I watched the fevered hedonism of the Thursday afternoon pool parties at the Dama Rose Hotel. That first week it was like every other start of a weekend. By lunchtime, women were rushing to hairdressers; the roads leading out of the city – those that were still open – were clogged with luxury cars. People who could do so were still heading outside the city to the villages, taking their kids to amusement parks, or en route to country villas for parties, weekend picnics or dinners.

Restaurants such as Narenj, which takes up nearly half a block in the Old City and served traditional Arabic food to the elite, were still packed. I went to a wedding there one afternoon, and was served plate after heaving plate of lamb, chicken, rice, dates, oranges and honey-drenched sweets. I was painfully aware that less than an hour away by car, assuming there were no roadblocks, people in Homs were starving to death, a massacre was going on in Houla, and refugees were crossing the borders of Lebanon, Turkey and Jordan searching for a way to feed their families.

The most surreal aspect of the Dama Rose parties was that they were taking place in the hotel, which was home to those 300 frozen, frustrated UN soldiers from fifty different countries, who had been brought in to be 'monitors'. On a top floor their boss, the Norwegian General Robert Mood, the chief monitor, was installed with his own team.

On 14 June 2012, their operations would be suspended because it became too dangerous for them. Eventually, most of them were pulled out, and a skeleton staff of UN workers remained behind – frustrated to the end with the encumbering politics.

Not for the first time, the UN was in an uncomfortable position. The UN is always an easy target for journalists and regional analysts. We like to mock their 'bloated inefficiency' (a favourite hackneyed term), and the often too obvious career aspirations of certain officials, which seem to come before their obligation to relieve human suffering. There is the cronyism, the preferential treatment of relatives and friends of senior officials, and vast corruption. But there are also a few committed officials, and more to the point, local field workers, who are determined to help people, to commit their lives, despite being hampered by the international institution's bureaucratic wrangles.

This time, the monitors, who wanted to be in Homs and Zabadani doing their job, were tethered to a hotel. They were on the fringe of a war they were unable to navigate or stop.

For the more honest senior officials, who spoke to me privately, there were deep anxieties that Syria was becoming another failure in the long list of catastrophes that included genocides in Bosnia, Rwanda and Sri Lanka, human trafficking in Kosovo, mass rape in the Congo (under the eyes of peacekeepers), and finally, cholera brought to Haiti in the aftermath of the 2010 earthquake.[1]

Veteran diplomats like Kofi Annan, Lakhdar Brahimi and Staffan de Mistura were brought in to negotiate with Assad and the rebels. Annan and Brahimi both quit, at an utter loss over what to do, and in the winter of 2015, de Mistura was still pushing on with a plan for 'freezing' local ceasefires in Aleppo, which, not surprisingly, never got off the ground.[2]

De Mistura, a veteran humanitarian, was determined to keep going, to relieve the unbearable suffering. It took a lot of persistence, after four years of war, to continue to try to forge some kind of path to peace.

The second week in June 2012, people were more sombre at the pool party. There was drinking, the house music blared, the UN staff still complained about the noise, but the Russian dancer was gone. And by the third week, people left early, rushing to their 4x4s with distinctly worried looks on their faces. No one wanted to be out after dark.

On the afternoon of 28 June, I could see that in the distance, towards the al-Marjeh neighbourhood, across from the Justice Courts, there was a larger than usual curl of smoke. Two car bombs had exploded earlier that day in the centre of Damascus. The day before had been the bloodiest day on record since the then sixteen-month uprising had begun. This Thursday, the partygoers were almost non-existent, and the ones who remained were decidedly less cheerful. There was music, but it was not blaring. There was no dancing. Most people were glued to their phones, texting family or friends for news or information.

2

Latakia – Thursday 14 June 2012

While I was lying on the floor, they stood over me, kicking me in the teeth and punching me and using their hands and feet. One man put his military boot in my mouth.

I lay there hiding my face as they kicked and thought: 'They are using my body to practise their judo moves.'

And the entire time they were beating me, they kept saying: 'You want freedom? Here's your freedom!' Every time they said freedom, they kicked or punched harder.

Then suddenly the mood changed. It got darker. They started saying if I did not talk, they would rape me.

The morning they came for her, Nada was still in her pyjamas. The air was cool from the night before, so she judged it to be around 6 a.m. She heard the muezzin call out for morning prayer, and heard her father – a welder who always got up in the early light – rising to pray.

For a moment, just when Nada opened her eyes, she tried to forget what the day might bring, imagining that her life was normal, as it had always been – before 2011, before the uprising.

Two days earlier, Nada had received a strange phone call. The number did not register on her caller ID. She stared at the monitor on her phone, then pressed the green button to accept the call.

'It's me,' he said, 'I'm in prison.'

She recognized the voice. It was a close friend, a colleague. Someone who also called himself an 'activist' like her. He had been picked up by Syrian state security and taken to the Central Prison in Latakia.

'Why are you calling me?' Nada asked, sitting down on the floor, the phone pressed to her ear. But she knew the answer, feeling her stomach turn over in fear.

'Can you get here right away?' he begged. 'Can you come to the police station? They want to talk to you, too.'

It was a signal they had practised since the war started.

It meant the police had caught him. He was probably being beaten, and was told to hand over the names of any fellow activists who were working against the Assad regime. Maybe they had smashed the bottom of his feet with a club, or attached his testicles to wires and turned on the electricity; maybe they had held his head under water until he thought his lungs would burst. Nada tried not to think of him, vulnerable, exposed, in pain. Crying.

Whatever had happened, he had probably cracked and given up Nada's name. But he had done her a favour by calling: it meant she had time to run.

She pressed the red button, ended the call, and drew herself into a tight small ball. She had nowhere to run. All she could do was wait.

Down the road from Nada's childhood home is the mountain town of Qardaha, the birthplace of Hafez al-Assad, the father of Bashar, who had ruled Syria for three decades. Hafez had been born poor, joining the Ba'ath Party as a student and later becoming a lieutenant in the Syrian Air Force. After the 1963 coup in Syria, which established Ba'athist military control over the country, Hafez al-Assad was put in charge of the Syrian Air Force. In 1966, after yet another coup, he was appointed as Minister of Defence. He gained mass popularity in domestic politics from that point on, allowing him later to overthrow Salah Jadid, Chief of Staff of the Armed Forces.

Hafez was born and buried in Qardaha. Upon his death in 2000, he was entombed in a white mausoleum next to his son Bassel, his intended successor, who had been killed in a car crash at thirty-two in 1994. His mother, Na'saa, rests down the road, shaded by a line of bowing trees.

Nada grew up in the Alawite triangle of Syria, and as a minority Sunni, always felt isolated. From relatives, she had heard stories of the Hama massacre in February 1982, of how the Syrian Army and the Defence Companies, under the orders of Hafez al-Assad, besieged the town of Hama for twenty-seven days in order to quell an uprising by the Muslim Brotherhood. Led by the Syrian Army, the siege effectively ended the anti-governmental campaign begun in 1976 by Sunni Muslim groups.

No one knows the exact number killed. Diplomats have reported 1,000, but other sources estimate that as many as 10,000 were slain. Nada was not sure of the number either, when I asked her.

Nada had grown up with these stories – and stories of the subsequent imprisonment and persecution of religious Sunnis – but her reasons for joining the opposition were not religious in nature. She joined because she 'wanted the chance to live in a democracy. As you do.'

In March 2011, as the Arab Spring was spreading in countries all around her, she first heard reports of unrest from the southwestern town of Daraa, just north of the border of Jordan, where the Syrian uprising began.

It started with kids, with graffiti. Fifteen kids, all from the same family, wrote anti-Assad slogans on the wall of their school. They were arrested, beaten, tortured and thrown into prison cells.

Every day, their families went to the local authorities, begging for news of their children. They received none. And from the silence of the jail cells to which Syrians had become so accustomed, finally came a spirit of rebellion. Perhaps it was fuelled by what was happening not far away in Tunisia, in Libya, in Egypt; but people who before had been afraid, and had remained submissive to the repression they had lived with for four decades, rose up. 'It was like watching people who were asleep suddenly wake up,' she said.

On 18 March, the beginning of spring, they gathered, hundreds of them, in front of the al-Omari mosque, and they chanted and cried, shouting for reforms: for an end to corruption, nepotism, unemployment, torture, security forces, secret police, paranoia. For an end to the lack of hope, lack of future, lack of political will. For a change from the life they had known under Assad. Within a week, there were thousands of people joined together.

But from the very beginning, Syrian security forces had been firing on the protesters. Three people were killed the first day. Two days later, seven policemen were killed, and four more protesters. The Syrian War had begun. While it was no surprise that it had started, what was surprising was how quickly it spread throughout the country: from Daraa to Homs, Hama to Aleppo, to Damascus and even to Latakia, the heart and soul of the Assad regime and of his Alawite minority.

Nada joined the opposition as a volunteer, willing to do anything to help. At first, she acted as a kind of runner. She brought medical supplies to the front lines, where opposition soldiers – not really soldiers, but rather her fellow students and friends – were fighting to overthrow Assad. She also made food – rice, vegetables, fruit – and delivered sandwiches. Then she began broadcasting reports of the opposition's message: their goals, their strategy.

It was extremely dangerous work, but important. People took notice of her, and finally, several months after the first shots were fired, she was promoted to chief of the local 'Revolution Media' department. Social media played a huge role in all of the Middle East uprisings, and Nada began to coordinate Facebook and Twitter accounts to help amplify the message of 'a democratic Syria'.

'I believed in what we were doing,' she said, 'and yes, I was afraid. We lived in a country where the security forces and the police were always something to be afraid of. It was hard to get that mentality – the one I had grown up with – out of my head, to try to live as though we really were going to be free.'

She had operated with her colleagues quietly for a year. She now realized that the authorities must have been watching her the entire time. She knew, as did her friends, that it was only a matter of time before they arrested her.

When Nada got off the phone that June morning in 2012, she sat on the floor for a moment and tried to arrange her thoughts. *Think*, she told herself. *Calmly*. She could run. But where would she go? What would she tell her family, who thought she was a student? And how would she get money, a passport and a plane ticket?

She decided to stay. 'I knew I could never outrun them. I had to face them.'

Her first thought was to destroy everything that might link her to the opposition. If she were caught, the rest of the operation would be compromised. She opened her mobile phone, took out the SIM card and shredded it. Then she went through the house, methodically finding and destroying every document, photograph, camera, notebook, memory stick – anything that might be considered evidence.

As she worked on autopilot, destroying her writings, her thoughts, her notes, she thought about what her father and mother would say when the police came for her. They knew nothing of her secret life. They had been excited for her when she became a part-time 'journalist'. But as she ripped up her notebooks and papers and went to the garden to make a small bin fire, she regretted nothing. She felt, as did so many others, that she was in the process of building a new country, a free one. Even as she was doing it, preparing for her last moments before her incarceration, she said she still believed it was the right thing to have done.

Two days later, everything had been destroyed. All Nada could do now was wait for them to come.

Everyone remembers their last morning of normality. The shaft of early morning light streamed through Nada's window onto her bed, making a small pool on her blanket. She remembers her mother's hurried knock on her door. She remembers the whiteness of her mother's face against her hijab and the tenseness of her mouth as she leaned over her daughter, still in bed, and whispered: 'There are six police cars outside; they are shouting out your name.'

Nada sat up and jumped out of bed. There was no time to escape now. She had just thought it would have taken longer for them to come for her.

Still in her pyjamas, she picked up her laptop from her desk and ran to the bathroom, locking the door. She sat on the cold floor, her head in her hands, until she heard them begin to knock, then pound, on the bathroom door.

'You have to open it, Farrah,' one of them said, using her *nom de guerre*. 'Open the door, Farrah. It's only wood. We can break it with one punch.'

They knocked again. And again.

Nada did nothing. She was frozen. She kept the laptop against her stomach, and rocked back and forth on the floor.

'Farrah? We're coming in.'

They kicked the door open easily, and found her on the floor.

Nada is tiny. Her bones are delicate, and her face is almost doll-like, with large blue eyes that make her seem younger than her twenty-five years. She covers her hair with a hijab, but the strands that escape are baby-fine, and a quiet brown.

One of the men half-lifted her off the ground. Nada weakly asked: 'May I get dressed?'

'Get dressed. Fast.'

She went to her room, heart pounding, and pulled on jeans and a sweater.

What Nada said she remembered most was the stupefied look on her parents' faces as she was forced into the police car. She walked willingly, but they opened the back door and thrust her inside the car. She looked back at her parents, as her father came forward, insisting that he had the right to accompany his daughter. He and the police argued. Nada hardly heard them, but her father eventually got into the car with her. He said nothing.

They drove to the military police station, and though he was silent, her father's presence soothed her. It was only to be a brief respite however, for once they arrived, the police ordered him to leave.

Her father said goodbye, and told her to be strong. 'As I saw my father go,' she remembers, 'I knew I was all alone and they could do anything they wanted.'

Hours later, after the beating had started, after the abuse and the sleep deprivation, after their kicks so fierce that they made her childish orthodontia dig into her gums and break her skin, after the gun butts to her head, face and kidneys became routine – she knew that she was entering a place from which, psychologically, she could never return.

★ ★ ★

The lowest depth that a human being can reach is to perform or to receive torture. The goal of the torturer is to inflict horrific pain and dehumanize another being. The act not only destroys both parties' souls – the victim's and the perpetrator's – but also the very fabric of a society. By subjecting men or women to enforced violence, sexual violation, or worse, you transform them into something subhuman. How does someone return to the human race after having been so brutalized?

By early 2012, reports began emerging of mass rape in Syria, on both sides of the conflict. In January, the International Rescue Committee's report included surveys from Syrian refugees in Lebanon and Jordan identifying rape as 'the primary reason their families fled the country'. The number two in charge at the UN's refugee agency, UNHCR, using the IRC report, claimed: 'Syria is increasingly marked by rape and sexual violence.'

While the crimes have been cited by both sides of the conflict, they seem to be perpetrated predominantly by President Bashar al-Assad's men, largely paramilitary agents known as Shabiha, or 'ghosts'.

Although Assad's own government troops were not always the perpetrators, the Shabiha did most of the dirty work when it came to sexual violence. Their tactics were largely to incite fear within communities – to enter towns or villages after the government troops had been fighting nearby, and spread the word that they would rape the women – daughters, mothers, cousins and nieces. Frightened, people would run, leaving scorched earth behind. It's a convenient way to ethnically cleanse an entire region. Fear can be generated so easily.

Sexual violence was not reported to be only against women either. There are many accounts of male rape, particularly in detention. Although prisons and detention centres were usually the most likely places for the crime to occur, it happened at checkpoints and when houses were being 'cleansed' as well.

Following the IRC report, videos began appearing on YouTube, as well as on Twitter and blogs, translating confessions of various captured Shabiha. The danger of such confessions is that some – such as that of the admitted rapist below – could not be verified as not having been given under great duress.

But the testimony given by a captured Shabiha is still chilling documentation.

Question: How long have you been with the security forces?

Response: Since the beginning of the revolution.

Question: What is your aim?

Response: To quash the revolution.

Question: And what else?

Response: We were induced by a certain amount of money.

Question: How much?

Response: Fifteen thousand Syrian pounds.

Question: Weekly? Monthly?

Response: Monthly.

Question: Do you go out to carry out raids?

Response: I go out on a security purpose.

Question: On a security purpose?

Response: Indeed, on a security purpose.

Question: With the army?

Response: Yes, and we raid the houses on the basis we are the security forces.

Question: Security forces?

Response: Indeed. We enter the houses to search. If there are men we push them out of the houses for a few hours. We take all the money and jewels we find. And if there are women, we rape them.

Question: How many women did you rape?

Response: Seven cases of rape.

Question: Seven?

Response: Indeed.

Question: Where did these rapes happen?

Response: Some at the village Al Fawl. First cases at the school, we raped them for six continuous hours. Then we entered another house as security forces on the ground that there are terrorists inside. We entered the house, we have tied the man, stolen jewels and money, and we raped women. One of them is from Knissat Bani Az. And we were four to rape her (me and three shabi-ha) and she committed suicide following her rape. The other case is a girl, we entered to search her house as security forces and we have stolen money and raped her. And there is another rape in Damascus. We entered her house on the ground we are security forces elements. We entered the house and raped the girl.

Question: And who did you deliver to the army?

Response: Five names.

Question: And who are the security forces you are dealing with?

Response: Lieutenant Colonel —.
Question: Who else?
Response: Two elements.
Question: Who is —?
Response: From the coast [the 'coast' being the Latakia region].

Whether or not rape is being used in Syria as a weapon of war needs to be further examined, but certainly it is a fear-provoking strategy. In February 2013, a United Nations report[3] for the Commission of Inquiry on Syria (COI) at the Human Rights Council stated: 'Syrian refugees . . . reported that one of the reasons that families fled was because of a perceived increased risk of kidnapping and rape.'

The findings below (from the same UN COI report) were based on forty-one interviews connected with sexual violence against men and women.

Between twenty and thirty soldiers and Shabiha – who she knew by name and who she described as 'Shias' from her village – entered her house looking for the men. Her aunt, three female cousins and three sisters-in-law were in the house, while the men were hiding in the basement. They beat the elderly aunt when she told them the men were in Lebanon. One of the Shabiha took two of her cousins upstairs to a separate room and locked the door while the others stayed downstairs. After the Shabiha left, the two stated that they had been beaten but she noticed the cousins couldn't walk properly afterwards and couldn't explain why they were separated from the rest if they had only been beaten.

While rape in any society is a horrific act of power and subjugation, in Muslim culture, it is devastating. Notions of virginity uphold the central concept of honour in Islam, not only for the victim, but also for the family. The COI reports cited five cases of women who had committed suicide after being raped. The crime was against women as young as fourteen.

'Sexual violence in Syria is not systematic – it's not like Rwanda where it was meant to wipe out a gene pool,' said Dr Zahra, a Syrian gynaecologist I met in 2013 on the Turkish–Syrian border who was working extensively with rape victims. 'But it is happening. It is happening every day.' There were an estimated 9,500 Syrians living in Antakya, where I saw Dr Zahra, at that time, after having fled their country.

'Not every woman who is arrested has been raped. Not all the women whose houses were raided were raped.' Zahra pauses. 'But the ones who have been are deeply traumatized.'

The girl had been abducted from the street by four men, two in military uniforms and two in civilian clothing. She was taken to an unknown building where she was kept and questioned by people she described as 'Shias from her neighbourhood'. While there she was interrogated by a woman about the work her mother did with the FSA [Free Syrian Army, the opposition].

During the interrogation, she was beaten with electrical wire, given injections . . . and had cigarettes extinguished on her chest. She was denied food and water for extended periods of time. On the fifth day of her detention, four young men were brought into the room, where they raped her. Two days later, she was released.

Her father took her to a gynaecologist outside Syria. In a separate interview, the doctor confirmed bruises, cigarette burns, injection marks on arms, and sexual injuries to the victim. This 14-year-old girl has tried to commit suicide three times, saying 'My life has no value. I lost everything, what has gone will never come back.'

United Nations COI report, February 2013

Nada's time had come.

The police (or perhaps the secret service or intelligence, she was not sure who they were) entered the room, sat down and looked at her as though she were a dog. One said abruptly: 'Talk or we will strip you!'

Nada, however, remained huddled on the floor, shaking with terror. 'I was like one of those little dogs, you know the kind that shake and shake and cannot stop shaking?'

She had never thought this would happen to her, never considered the potential consequences if she got caught working with the opposition. 'I just did it. I did not think – maybe I did not let myself think – of what could happen.'

Still, Nada did not cry, at least not at first. She just lay on the ground wishing she were dead.

Eight months and three days is a horrifically long time to be held captive and tortured. And the pain wasn't just physical. Perhaps the worst part was that her jailers delighted in telling her that her family had been notified she was dead.

In fact, Nada spent her days and nights in a dirty cell not far from her childhood home, but the people she loved most in the world were grieving for her. They believed her body was no longer of this earth. She felt invisible. She felt alone. The psychological torture was more terrifying than the physical abuse.

'To think that the outside world, the people that love you think you are dead when in fact you are alive . . .'

A small, dark cell became Nada's home for eight months. Nada's cell was not even big enough for her already small frame to stretch out in; she remained curled up. The jeans she wore throughout the entire ordeal are still creased in the areas of her body which she was unable to move.

'I kept them,' she says. 'To remember what they did to me.'

In one corner of the cell, there was a hole – an Arabic toilet – and a water tap. 'I kept the water running all the time because I was afraid of rats coming up the drainpipe and biting me.' She could not sleep, and when she did, she dreamed of those same rats covering her body. She would wake up crying and screaming, clutching her body to protect herself from the imaginary rodents.

Other men and women were kept in the cells next to her own. She did not know who they were, but they too would scream out, crying, pleading for mercy, for an end to the torture. Some cried for their mothers.

'This was part of my torture,' she says. 'To hear other people begging, and to know they were coming for me next. When they would stop in front of my door and turn the key – my heart would stop.'

She tried to keep track of time, but it was impossible as her body wasted away. She imagined herself disappearing. Her family too. She had no news of them, nor of her friends, nor of her other captured colleagues. They told her that other activists had betrayed her, that Assad had won the war, and that the opposition was dead. 'I sank into a dark place.'

When she asked for water, they would bring a male prisoner, make him urinate into a bottle, and try to force her to drink it. When she spat it out, they would throw it back in her face. The male prisoner, equally humiliated, would avoid her eyes.

'I remember every single one of their faces,' she says bitterly of her tormentors, of that memory. 'I will look for them. I AM looking for them.'

The stripping led to beatings. The beatings led to further abuse.

She was relentlessly interrogated for names, dates and occasions where she met her fellow Syrian Youth Union colleagues.

There was always at least one interrogator, sometimes more. She would sit; they would circle her like wolves.

She was continually threatened with rape.

'They would say "Talk or we will strip you",' she says, covering her eyes with the swipe of a hand. 'That was their line, their threat.'

One day, when she was not telling them what they wanted to hear, they brought her to an all-male cell where the prisoners were in their underwear.

The men stared at her lustfully. She was one of them, but they were men, and they had been locked up a long time.

'It was horrible,' she says. 'Humiliating. They told me they would leave me with these hungry men and they would take care of me.' She felt like a rabbit surrounded by wolves.

'I am a conservative Muslim woman, I thought I was being given to these men for them to rape me,' she said. 'And so I started screaming. I think I screamed for three hours. Until my throat was stripped raw. They wanted to break me. And they did. Finally, I said, "Okay, I will tell you the truth".'

She said she talked. She told them things. But what she told them was not enough. After several hours, they moved her – the first of many moves – and brought her to a place that she calls 'the horror room'. The room was only as wide as 'a man's body'. They tied her hands to an iron bar behind her back.

Then a man entered with a whip. 'Every time I said something he did not like,' she says, beginning to break into sobs, 'he whipped me.'

Her bloodied and bruised body was then handed over to another interrogator, who was told, 'Okay, now really take care of her.'

'Now the real beatings began,' she says sombrely, 'and the terrible things.'

For more than four years, I roamed refugee camps, safe houses, cities and towns in Lebanon, Egypt, Turkey, Jordan, Syria, Kurdistan and Iraq, talking to women who had been raped during the war. Initially I did it as a journalist and analyst; later I worked for the United Nations Refugee Agency (UNHCR) working on reports about Syrian women who were left alone owing to the war, and were susceptible to sexual predation.

They were hard to find, these women, for most direct victims did not wish to talk with me. I often had to rely on friends or family, who would whisper about such-and-such a woman, and I would do my best to track them down. I never forced them to talk, and if they did not want to see me, I did not push them. I believed they had suffered enough.

Eventually, working near the Turkish–Syrian border in 2013, I was told about a 'safe' house in Northern Syria, near Aleppo, where nearly a dozen women were hiding. All had allegedly been raped by Shabiha, and were being tended to and cared for by a religious woman. But when I finally tracked the safe house down, they had moved – the women were not safe, and they had gone to another village.

Once I had identified the victims, and if they agreed to talk to me, I still had to decipher their language of shame. I tried to explain that I was not going to identify them or expose their terrible secret, and that speaking might, in some way, eventually bring the perpetrators to justice. That was the singular motive of the women – and the men – who agreed to talk to me: that the men who had done this to them would not be able to walk the streets when the war was finished, with impunity. Some told me they spoke to me because hiding their story was like a 'stone weighing down my heart', as one young girl said tearfully.

Many years before, I had had a similar task in Bosnia and Kosovo. Following those wars, the women were often held in 'rape camps' for weeks or even months, and would not use the word 'rape' in their own language. They would say – between sobs – that they had been 'touched'. They would cry, saying that if their husbands knew, they would divorce them to find a clean woman. They covered up their secret like a bloody wound, and told no one.

The taboo of rape for any woman is enormous. But for a Muslim woman, who is meant to be a virgin upon marriage, it is the end of life, or the life she was meant to live. If she was single before, she will probably never marry. She will not have children, a family. In other cultures, this might be fine; but in the Middle East, where large families are a given, it means isolation from the rest of society.

Later, Yazidi women, from an ancient community in northern Iraq, would report being kidnapped by ISIS soldiers, sold into slavery, held in houses, raped, forced to marry their captors. The sexual violence used against women during the war that rages through Syria (and later, Iraq, when ISIS pushed through the town of Mosul and began to erase the borders between Syria and Iraq) is a way of fighting the men themselves: if we cannot fuck you, we will fuck your women.

Most of the rapes I was able to document were committed in detention. Some happened at checkpoints. Other women were raped in their homes, when the Shabiha entered their villages.

The women who were held in detention report that rape was always the threat used when they were not 'cooperating'. One young woman said that she was imprisoned with her mother and forced to watch the soldiers beating her mother.

'I did not care what they did to me,' she said, 'but to see my mother suffering . . .' The soldiers threatened to rape her mother, before telling the mother that they were going to rape the daughter.

'This was the most terrible psychological pressure. I do not think you can imagine the pain . . .'

Another young woman in Aleppo told me she was arrested for putting up revolutionary posters. She was partially stripped, blindfolded and tied to a chair.

'Then they said they would pass me from man to man.'

When I met Nada in a safe house in southern Turkey, she had been out of prison for some months. But she still had the reflexes of a prisoner, of someone huddling in a corner, protecting her face and her body from blows. Sudden movements made her jump; she would frequently get lost in her thoughts, and stay silent for several minutes, or well up with tears.

She was minuscule in size, thinner than when she had entered prison, which made it hard for me to believe that anyone could beat her with a stick or a whip. She looked as though she would break in two if you touched her. Her body was the size of a twelve-year-old: no breasts, no hips, shoulders hardly wide enough to carry her frame. She wore a lavender hijab and a tight red sweater. The childish clash of colours seemed to emphasize how young she looked.

When we first met, she cowered when I touched her hand in greeting. She seemed broken, vulnerable. She would not use the word rape. She told her story in staccato. But after a while of sitting quietly, her face changed into a myriad of emotions – sadness, pain, then the heavy flood of memory, and finally revulsion. She told of the day they brought in a male prisoner and forced her to watch him being sodomized. As she talks, her voice deadened, she opens and closes her hand mechanically, clutching at the straps of her backpack. She starts to cry. It very quickly turns to a raw sobbing.

'The things I saw . . . the things I saw . . .' she spits out. 'It is unbearable to explain what I saw . . . *I cannot forget . . . I saw . . . another prisoner being raped . . . a man being raped. I heard it . . . I saw it . . . Do you know what it's like to hear a man cry?*'

She abruptly gets up from the chair where she is sitting, claps a hand over her mouth, and runs into a nearby bathroom. She turns on the tap and begins to vomit.

A friend, who is with her, is also close to tears.

'Yes, Nada was raped,' she says. 'But she can never admit it, even to herself.'

Her friend goes to console her. She comes back. 'She cannot even say the word aloud. When she talks of others and what they endured,' her friend says, 'she is talking about what happened to her.'

There are no words to say to her, no more details to extract. What has happened to Nada cannot be undone. What she has seen and heard cannot be forgotten. It cannot be erased.

A few days later, I offered Nada and a friend a ride in my car to a class in Antakya. They were studying English together, taking a course that Nada hopes will eventually get her a job, and maybe a chance at a new life. When her friend talks about this, Nada offers a fleeting smile, and looks, if only for a moment, like any other young woman her age setting out into life – confident, happy, free.

Then something crosses her mind, and her eyes go grey and dead once again.

'I changed a lot when I was in prison,' she says quietly. Then she smiles. 'But you know, even there, I was the revolutionary.'

In between beatings and interrogation sessions, she confronted her jailers. She chastised them for small things, for prisoners' rights. It gave her a feeling of having some control.

'I made them get plates for the other prisoners!' she says proudly. 'I made them realize we are not just dogs to be kicked and used, but people. I made them put plastic over the broken windows.' She looks faintly triumphant. 'Before we had nothing, then we got plates!'

Small victories for a broken spirit.

One afternoon in Antakya, a friend introduced me to Shaheeneez, a thirty-seven-year-old former teacher. She was dressed in black trousers and a long black belted coat, despite the heat. She wanted to meet somewhere anonymous. When she entered the room, a shadow seemed to walk alongside her.

After she sat, Shaheeneez explained that she is very religious. As she talked, I couldn't help but notice her headscarf, silver rings and watch, her olive, faintly pitted skin, her full nose and defined jawline. She looked strong rather than pretty.

Still, she was nervous and jittery, visibly shaking as she spoke. When I learned that it was only recently that she had got out of a Syrian jail in which she had been held for 'several months', I began to understand why.

As she told it, in 2012 she was arrested at the airport on her way to Egypt from her home in Aleppo. She was going to a conference. 'I think my name was on some kind of list.' Her actual arrest was probably for political activities, but she is not sure.

After she was taken, the men who arrested her threw her into a state security prison in Damascus. There she was blind-folded and interrogated, often for hours at a time.

'It confused me,' she said, trying to explain what it was like to be asked questions with her eyes covered. 'I heard voices, but could not put the faces to them. It was a tactic, made to scare me more.'

The interrogation exhausted her, but she had no intention of giving away names. She was aware of what they were trying to do to get her to confess. At one point, the interrogators changed their tactics; their voices grew rougher and they began to hit her. One wallop knocked her to the floor. While she was on the ground, they tied her hands together. She remembered how the rope cut into her skin. One of the men hovered over her. Someone tugged at her clothes. She heard a door open, close.

'That is where they abused . . .' she stumbled over the word, '. . . me.'

She said they kept her on the floor. They partially removed her clothes.

'They said they would do terrible things if I did not cooperate . . .' Shaheeneez's shoulders began to shake under her dark coat.

'They said rape . . . then I was on the floor... then I felt something hard inside me . . .'

She paused now in this room far from where it actually happened, but she was still trembling, and she moved to the window. She opened it, turned her face towards the sunlight, her back to the room. She seemed to gulp air.

'They raped me,' she said. She said it again. Then all the breath went out of her.

Afterwards, Shaheeneez cried for a long time while I sat opposite her. I was unable to say anything that would console her. I laid a hand on her shoulder; she flinched at the touch. The tears rolled off her face onto her collar.

She said she had been seeing a psychiatrist since the violation, but it didn't help. At the time, she had been in love. She had plans to get married and had a life mapped out in front of her.

Her doctor urged her to tell her fiancé the truth. But when she did, he left her. 'He said he could not marry me, that he had to find a clean woman,' she said, adding that it is more than a feeling of being violated, it's one of being completely ruined.

'But I don't think the interrogators did the actual rape. I think that man who entered the room did.' She sat on the bed, sweating and shaking. 'I think it took them less than half an hour. And then, after they untied me and took off my blindfold, I found blood on my legs.' She did not know whether the 'hard thing' was an object they used to penetrate her, or a penis.

She had been a virgin.

Shaheeneez seems as damaged as Nada, but is even less able to cope and continue living. While neither woman will forget what happened, Nada says she wants to move on, to find a new path forward. But Shaheeneez says she cannot forget. The rape, she says, destroyed her life.

'If I get engaged again,' she says, 'I will never tell him.'

★ ★ ★

A few days later, I was working inside Atma Camp, the largest internally displaced camp in Syria at that time, home to 50,000 displaced and miserable souls. I was searching for a woman called Rana, who was trying to help a group of other Syrian refugee women who had been raped. In technical terms, they are called 'survivors'.

As far as refugee camps go, Atma was well organized. As far as living goes, it was hellish.

When I found the camp doctor – a young man working in the camp who spoke halting English – and told him what I was investigating, he looked anguished. I had not used the word rape, only 'sexual violence'.

'In Syria, the innocent people suffer the most,' he responded, finally. 'Do you really find women who have been touched? For us, this is the worst thing to do to the men – because they are our women.'

We climbed down a hill, passing the water stations that had been set up as showers and sinks. Only a dozen water stations for hundreds and hundreds of people.

We then realized that a tiny boy was following us. He looked like an ordinary kid, about the age of my own nine-year-old, hiding his face behind a blue hoodie. He was wearing fake G-star jeans.

But then I saw his face: it was completely burnt. His mouth appeared to be nothing more than a hole and his nose was practically non-existent. His ears were flaps of skin, which had been stretched tight into pink crevasses, across his skull.

I asked him his name. It was Abdullah and he told me he was eleven years old.

Even with the doctor as my guide, I didn't find the raped women in Atma. They had been moved. But later, I saw Abdullah again, standing in front of a refugee tent. It was his home.

His parents invited me inside; they told me how he was injured at home in the city of Hama last October.

It was a clear day: good weather for bombing. When the bombs came that day, Abdullah was playing on his computer. It was always so difficult to keep the children occupied inside, his mother says. Hearing the crash of bombs, Abdullah – in his fear – ran outside.

He got the full impact of the bomb that landed near his house.

'I heard the worst thing in the world that day of the bombing,' the father said. 'The sound of my own son's screams of pain.'

He looked at Abdullah, who stared back at him with confusion.

Then he said something that both Nada and Shaheeneez also said to me – the mantra their jailers tormented them with. It is the battle cry of the activists, the first demonstrators in Daraa, filtering down to all the Syrian cities, the provinces, and villages: We Want Freedom.

Abdullah's father turned towards his son's raw face. He asked: 'So is this freedom?'

3

Ma'loula and Damascus –
June–November 2012

I was in Ma'loula, watching the morning prayers of a group of solemn nuns, a quiet and reflective moment, when I heard about the car bombs back in Damascus. Ma'loula is an ancient mountaintop town dug into a cliff, renowned for its spiritual healing qualities and restorative air. It was a place I felt drawn to: something of an oasis of tolerance. The residents were mainly Christian – it is one of the last places where Western Aramaic, the language of Jesus Christ, is still spoken – and they vowed at the beginning of the Syrian conflict not to succumb to sectarianism and be dragged into the chaos.

Their determination was all the more remarkable given the town's location. It lies on the main road at an equal distance between Homs and Damascus. It was a defiant place, but their defiance reflected a bitter history.

Ma'loula was besieged during the Great Syrian Revolt in 1925, when rebel Druze, Christians and Muslims tried to throw off the colonial oppression of France. The history of that insurrection lingers. Many older residents were weaned on stories of women and children hiding in the caves of the three mountains that surround the town, to escape atrocities.

The Christians are largely from the Greek Catholic and Antiochian Orthodox offshoots; the Muslims are Sunnis. But most people would not classify themselves by religion, preferring to say simply, 'I am from Ma'loula.'

That morning, I had awoken early in Damascus and drove with my friend, Maryam, a Sunni from Damascus, to Ma'loula, about an hour away. We left our car, and began to walk up and down the streets. There was serenity in the shaded courtyards edged with olive and poplar trees that calmed me after the chaos and noise of Damascus. Maryam described how she had come as a small girl, and watched the nuns go about their daily tasks in a quiet and humble way, making apricot jam, or polishing the candlesticks in the chapel.

Maryam had a friend, the Sunni imam of the town, Mahmoud Diab. She knocked at his door with some hesitation and asked if we could come inside for tea, and to talk to him. He opened the door, asking us to put on our head-scarves, and led us to chairs under the flowering trees. Even in his courtyard, there was still a fading poster of Assad attached to the wall. 'Do you still support him?' I asked.

Diab looked surprised. 'Of course,' he said.

We sat quietly for a few moments waiting for our tea. He pointed out the sounds of the birds. I asked him how Ma'loula remained so peaceful.

'Early on in this war, I met with the main religious leaders in the community: the bishop and the mother superior of the main convent,' Diab said. 'We decided that even if the mountains around us were exploding with fighting, we would not go to war.'

Diab had not been born and raised in Ma'loula, but was educated here, married here. He was, at that time, also in the Syrian Parliament. He was a Sunni, he said, but that did not mean he wanted his city to be torn to bits.

'It's a sectarian war, in politics it's another name,' he said with a shrug. 'But the fact is, there is no war here in Ma'loula. Here, we all know each other.'

Tolerance had been a tradition in Ma'loula since St Takla – the daughter of a pagan prince, an early disciple of St Paul, and possibly even his wife – had fled to these mountains in the first century AD. She was escaping from soldiers sent by her father, who threatened to kill her for her religious beliefs.

The legends – and the old people – say Takla was exhausted and finding her way blocked by the sharp, rocky sides of a mountain, she fell on her knees in desperate prayer. The mountains parted. 'Ma'loula' means 'entrance' in Aramaic.

'Here in these mountains are all different people, different religions. But we decided adamantly that Ma'loula would not be destroyed,' Diab said.

At the ancient shrine of St Takla, Christian nuns – true believers in the Assad government – lived isolated, quiet lives, devoted to God and country. They slept in small, spotlessly clean chambers and passed their time working, praying and tending to the needs of the sick. They also ran an orphanage.

The convent was silent except for constant, shrill birdsong and the sound of nuns scurrying up and down marble stairs with large glass jars of the golden-coloured fruit, which they made and sold. They would dry the apricots in boxes in the courtyard, and the scent of the hot fruit was as heavy as the incense in the chapel.

The convent is one of forty holy sites in Ma'loula, which before the war was a place where Muslims and Christians prayed to cure infertility or other ailments, and drank water from the crack in the rock that St Takla is said to have parted with her prayers.

But religion is not an issue, said Mother Sayaf, a Greek Catholic who has lived in this convent for thirty years. She spoke to me in a quiet, completely darkened room – shuttered from the fierce light – and one of the younger nuns brought glasses of iced water on a lacquered tray. She said the air was so fresh that Ma'loula was a place where doctors sent sick people to recuperate.

'We had an Iraqi Muslim man who was badly wounded, who came here to be healed,' she said, meaning they would treat someone regardless of religion. At the same time, she made no secret of her devotion to Assad. Two years later, when the jihadists entered Ma'loula, her devotion to the regime would be tested.

I returned several times to Ma'loula to visit the monastery and the nuns. When I last went, in November 2012, as people fled embattled Homs, Damascus and Aleppo to seek refuge with relatives overseas or in the few still peaceful parts of Syria, people were returning to Ma'loula as a sort of safe haven.

'It's my country,' said Antonella, a Syrian-American who left Los Angeles and Miami three years ago to return to her birthplace and start a café. She sat down inside her café – no electricity – and showed me maps. She reminded me Ma'loula was a UNESCO-protected heritage site, which she felt would somehow exclude them from being blown to bits.

Antonella had a chance to leave when the war started and fighting was close to Ma'loula, but refused. 'I want to be here,' she said. Her business, however, was suffering; money was a problem and she had an elderly mother she needed to support.

Ma'loula did look different in the past, she said. 'There were fifty tour buses a day here when I first came back,' she said. Her café, which was empty the day I sat with her, was once full. She wasn't sure how she was going to get through the next winter.

The previous year, when there was fighting in Yabroud, a strategically located town near the Lebanese border and just across the mountain, Antonella finally realized her country was at war and people were dying. 'That depressed me,' she says. 'The truth is, even if Ma'loula is quiet now, no one knows where this is going.'

But she still stoically supported Assad. 'The rebels have destroyed our country,' she said. There was no other alternative.

Her brother Adnan, who had also come back from America, sat down and began to talk about the economy. Because of sanctions and the fact that transit has been halted across borders – trucks couldn't move because of fighting in certain areas – food costs were skyrocketing. Foreign tourists had stopped coming. People bought only what was necessary. Small businesses, like Antonella's, were dying.

'This is the beginning of World War III,' predicted Adnan. 'It is starting in Syria, but it will engulf the region. This is a proxy war.'

I wandered back up the hill to say goodbye to Diab, the imam. I wanted to ask him one more question. Can a town renowned for its tolerance resist the centrifugal pressures of a vicious, sectarian civil war?

'Everyone is a Christian and everyone is Muslim,' he answered diplomatically, not really answering the question. He refused to break down the percentage of Muslims. 'It does not matter,' he insisted. 'The situation here will not deteriorate. It's the opposite. People support each other.'

'If we become Salafist,' he said, referring to the fundamentalist strain of Islam that has taken on a new prominence in the Arab Spring, 'we lose all of this ethnic mix, and that is tragic. Everyone has to be like them. There is no room for anyone else.'

On 4 September 2013, a Jordanian suicide bomber exploded a truck at a Syrian Army checkpoint at the entrance to Ma'loula. Rebels then attacked the checkpoint – the explosion was assumed to have been a signal – killing eight soldiers and taking control of several sections of the historical town. The Syrian Army led a counter-attack two days later, regaining control of the town, but continuing to battle against jihadists in the surrounding area. But the rebels, having received reinforcements, once again took the town, allegedly burning down some churches and harassing the town's Christian residents. According to some sources, nearly the entire population of this diverse town had fled, leaving only about fifty people inside its limits. The army eventually conquered the rebels and secured Ma'loula on 15 September, and many residents returned, but they still lived in fear of further attack.

In late November, opposition forces again attacked Ma'loula, this time kidnapping twelve nuns from the monastery in order to ransom the women in exchange for their own prisoners of war. On 14 April 2014, the Syrian Army, with the help of Hezbollah, once more took control of Ma'loula.

Recalling the events, sixty-two-year-old Adnan Nasrallah said: 'I saw people wearing al-Nusra headbands who started shooting at crosses.' One of them 'put a pistol to the head of my neighbour and forced him to convert to Islam by obliging him to repeat "there is no God but God". Afterwards they joked, "He's one of ours now".'

In late February 2015, Christians in Ma'loula prayed for their fellow Christians, hundreds of whom had been kidnapped and murdered by the Islamic State of Iraq and the Levant.

On the road back to Damascus that afternoon in 2012, long before the Salafists arrived, we saw the first signs of war getting closer to Ma'loula. As we approached Damascus, smoke rose, curling into the skyline. A car bomb. The sun bore down on the car, in contrast to the cool convent with its sense of hushed protection. The traffic was stalled for miles at the roadblocks, so we left our car by the side of the road and walked to the bombsite.

It stank of burnt rubber. Skeletons of charred cars remained. No one had been hurt, which was fortunate. The explosion was caused by 'sticky bombs' – handmade bombs taped to the bottom of a car, which had been parked just across from the Justice Courts at the height of the rush hour.

'Real amateur hour,' one UN official said to me later. 'The bombers didn't know what they were doing – it's just a scare tactic to make the people hate the opposition.'

For a while, it worked. People blamed the opposition and 'foreign interventionists' for the explosions. Crowds of people gathered, angry that their city was quickly falling victim to the devastation that was spreading across the country.

'Our only friend is Russia!' one well-dressed man shouted near the bombsite, his face contorted with rage. 'These are foreigners that are exploding our country! Syria is for Syrians!'

It was a common belief that the bombs and the chaos that were spreading throughout the country were widely being caused by a 'third element'. This was especially true in Damascus, which had long been an Assad stronghold. People refused to believe that the opposition could rule their country without turning it into a Salafist kingdom, an Islamic caliphate where women were not allowed out of the house and Christians were locked up and sold as slaves.

This was nearly a year before we even began to hear about ISIS, the Islamic State.

A crowd gathered around us. People were getting agitated from the heat, from the uncertain future, from the violence that had just ripped through their streets. My driver wanted to go.

After we had returned to the hotel, I watched the end of the pool party in the dying light of the day, and against the faint dusk I could still see the grey, acrid smoke plumes curling in the air, a warning sign of darker days to come.

'Look at what happened in Tunisia, look at what happened in Libya, look at the results of Egypt,' said Ahmed, a wealthy seventeen-year-old in a pink Lacoste shirt, faded jeans and Nikes. He was agitated and passionate: he wanted to talk to someone who was not Syrian and he did not often have the chance. 'Listen to me! Everyone thinks we are the bad guys, that Assad is a monster. But there is another side to the story.'

Ahmed was giving me a ride home from a dinner party in Damascus – his mother had asked him to take me. 'He has some solid ideas on politics,' she said. 'He expresses what all of us think.' So Ahmed got the car keys and drove me through the winding streets, back to my hotel.

Ahmed was from a wealthy family and went to a good school in Damascus, where he lived in a comfortable villa with his family. He was leaving shortly to do his military service in the Syrian Army, then to study at an American university.

The dinner that night had included Ahmed's mother, his grandmother, his aunts and his cousin – all of whom are highly educated, multilingual and the holders of several passports. It's a common thread with the elite in Damascus – to be bi-national, to have a second passport, a way out. When I pointed out that this might be the reason that they supported Assad – because if it all went wrong, they had a place to flee – Ahmed's mother looked at me darkly. 'We had years of French occupation, coups, years of Ba'athists,' she said. 'Now we do not want the years of Islamists.'

After dinner, we sat on the balcony amongst flowering jasmine plants, smoking apple-flavoured shisha. Ahmed sat in a wicker chair. 'I am one hundred per cent behind the government – not that I believe everything Assad is doing is right,' he said, 'but because the time is not right for change and it should not be imposed by the West.'

'Syria is geopolitically important,' he added. 'People want to get their hands on it. And why should we take democracy lessons from Saudi Arabia, which arms the opposition?' Saudi Arabia, he reminded me, 'did not let women drive'.

The party did not break up until after midnight, and we went out into the street. There was no curfew. People were still out on the streets, walking home from dinners or from visits with family. We passed a bank of floodlights on a street corner: a commercial was being filmed in the middle of a country that had just declared civil war.

'Life goes on,' Ahmed said.

There was a crowd of people watching the shoot, and a few actors were waiting for their call. I saw an actress named Dima, whom I had met at the hotel the day before while she was dressing up in Gucci and Christian Louboutin heels for a magazine photo shoot. The shoes, she pointed out, were a brand that was a favourite of the President's wife, Asma al-Assad.

In an interview with Asma for US *Vogue* entitled 'A Rose in the Desert', the journalist Joan Juliet Buck praised the beauty and philanthropy of Asma al-Assad, wife of the dictator. The piece had unwisely been published in the magazine's March 2011 'Power' issue, just as the Arab Spring was erupting in the Middle East. It caused a storm of criticism and was pulled off *Vogue*'s website in May 2011, as it became clear how many people the government was willing to kill to remain in power.

Buck later said she had been pressured not to mention politics to the Assads. In other words, reading between the lines, she was not to counter the glowing references to Asma's beauty with the fact that her husband's father's regime had killed thousands of people in three weeks to wipe out Muslim extremists (in the Hama massacre in 1982). And that Asma's husband was now basically doing the same.

Like Asma, Dima wanted to be in *Vogue*. She was sitting in a chair near the window being made up when I first saw her: like Asma, she was stunning: alluring eyes and strong bone structure. Dima saw me and smiled, motioned for me to come in: she spoke good English and wanted news of the world.

'Not of war,' she said. 'Please don't talk of war. Talk of the world. What's happening out there? I want to go to New York, to California . . .' She wanted to hear about Kanye West and Kim Kardashian; about films showing in cinemas where there was no war; about music and magazines and dresses.

That night with Ahmed, Dima spotted me in the car, and called me over. 'Do you want to come and watch?' she asked. 'We just started filming.'

Behind her, looming slightly, were two burly men in leather jackets. One of them motioned for her to come back after she talked to me, and she obeyed, head bent. She looked solemn as they spoke. Then she approached our car again. She was no longer friendly.

'Maybe you'd better go,' she said. 'It's late. I'll call you tomorrow. We can drink coffee or something.'

'Who are those men? Your bodyguards?'

She looked at them to make sure they were not listening, and then cupped her hands around my ear, as if telling a little girl a secret. She shook her head.

'They are Shabiha,' she said. 'Just go home.'

Damascus has two faces.

There are the opposition activists who are working day and night on their computers, and sometimes in the streets, to bring down Assad. These are the ones who meet me in secret, the ones who disappear from their offices one day, like Mazen Darwish, a lawyer who founded a group promoting free expression, or Razan Zeitouneh, another human rights activist. These are the ones who risk going to jail for up to forty-five days' detention (same as the old French mandate administrative detention law, being held without charges) and the ones who simply seem to have no fear. Even peaceful protesters have been thrown in jail simply for demonstrating, without their families being told of their whereabouts.

By 2015, it was difficult to calculate the number of missing and detained in Syria after four years of conflict. But Bassam al-Ahmad from the Violations Documentation Center told me: 'Those we can document by name, we believe to be 36,000 held by the regime, and around 1,200 by ISIS. But if we are talking about estimated figures, we are sure that the numbers are bigger.' The Syrian Organization for Human Rights gave a higher figure.

The President of the International Federation of Human Rights, Karim Lahidji, told me the conditions for detainees, especially the political prisoners, are terrible: 'In the jails of the regime, torture and abuse are the norm. The overwhelming majority are arbitrarily detained.'

'I have worked in many countries where torture has been a significant problem, but, quite frankly, I struggle to remember a place where torture has been so widespread and systematic,' said Ole Solvang from Human Rights Watch. 'The Syrian government is running a virtual archipelago of torture centres scattered around the country.'

The other face of Syria was not an archipelago of torture. This was Damascus, party time: people drinking champagne in Narenj, the fancy Damascus restaurant, or getting married in tight sparkly dresses with low-cut backs and holding elaborate parties at Le Jardin Restaurant with Druze musicians, or filmmakers doing high-end commercials with actors who were not in prison.

'This is how I see it: *We don't want our world to change.* I'm still jogging and swimming every day,' Rida, a well-off, sixty-four-year-old businessman said one afternoon over lunch. 'This is *not* a war. Our regime is strong. Seventy per cent are fully supporting Assad.'

'You don't want your world to change, but for some people, it has changed without their consent,' I said. 'They are getting bombed or tortured or shot at.'

'This is the bias of the press,' he retorted.

His wife, Maria, who wore a headscarf and went to the Opera nearly every week, agreed. 'When the FSA [the Free Syrian Army] comes and tells people to close their shops and protest against the government, they burn them down if the people refuse,' she said. 'This is why I am supporting the government.'

'Are you frightened?' I asked. 'Will your world change?'

'Not at all,' says Rida. 'Last week we had a party of twenty people on our balcony. We were all relaxing and smoking the shisha. We heard gun shots in the background – but it seemed a long way off.'

During the years I spent in Syria, I twice went to the opera house, which is said to be the second-grandest in the Middle East. Once I went with Maria and Rida. The second time I went to meet the director. She did not want me to use her name.

'I do not want to give the impression that we are like the *Titanic* – the orchestra plays on while the ship sinks,' she said. We were sitting in her office and she motioned overhead with a hand gesture then put her finger to her lips, meaning that the room was probably bugged, although I am not sure what music has to do with state security.

I told her that there was a cellist who played Albinoni's 'Adagio' over and over in the ruins of the National Library of Sarajevo during the siege from 1992 to 1995. She mentioned the Russian musicians playing during the siege of Leningrad, with the performance of Shostakovich's Symphony no. 7 broadcast over loudspeakers, much to the anger of the Germans besieging them.

'Music and art in times like these fuel the soul,' she said. 'It gives people hope.' To get to the concerts, people had to pass checkpoints at night, a time when it is not necessarily safe to go out.

She told me that, unlike Rida and Maria, she was scared. 'People are leaving, people are packing up and going to Europe or Lebanon.' In the summer heat, she shivered. 'This is my country! How can I go?'

It was not long after our meeting that I heard she too had fled, leaving her prestigious job and the second-best opera house in the Middle East and moving to Paris.

But one morning, while she was still in Syria, she invited me to see the Children's Orchestra practising. They were led by a visiting British conductor. She was proud that he had come 'in these times'.

Some of the musicians were very young – around eight, with tiny hands holding their instruments. But others looked like teenage kids from anywhere else – Brazilian surfing bracelets, baggy jeans, long flowing hair. They practised a powerful song of innocence, 'Evening Prayer' from Humperdinck's fairy-tale opera *Hansel and Gretel*.

When at night I go to sleep
Fourteen angels watch do keep
Two my head are guarding
Two my feet are guarding

Two are on my right hand
Two are on my left hand
Two who warmly cover,

Two who o'er me hover
Two to whom 'tis given
To guide my steps to heaven
Sleeping softly, then it seems
Heaven enters in my dreams;
Angels hover round me,

Whisp'ring they have found me;
Two are sweetly singing
Two are garlands bringing,
Strewing me with roses
As my soul reposes,
God will not forsake me
When dawn at last will wake me.

I sat for a good while watching the fresh, young faces intently reading the musical scores and holding their instruments with something akin to first love. I wondered what this room would look like if I returned exactly this time a year later. How many of these boys would be sent for mandatory military service? How many would flee the country? I tried not to ask myself if any would no longer be living.

They begin to play again, at the urging of the conductor. As I watched and listened, I grew emotional and I thought of the words that I had often sung to my son when he was a tiny baby in his crib. It is a song of protection, of reassurance, of love. But I could already feel that no one was protecting Syria, there were no angels, and that perhaps God had forsaken them.

Maria Saadeh's last name translates from the Arabic as 'happiness'. She lives in Star Square, in the old French mandate section of Damascus, in an old 1920s building that she helped to renovate. A restoration architect by training, educated in Syria and France, she had recently been elected, without any experience, as the only Christian independent female parliamentarian.

The Christians are anxious. On Sundays during my stay, I go to their churches — Eastern Christian or Orthodox — and watch them kneel and pray. I smell the intense aroma of beeswax, and see fear on their faces. It reminds me of being at mass in Mosul (which would be overrun by ISIS forces on 10 June 2014, causing its Christian population to scatter) before the American invasion in 2003. Fear, mixed with faith. Trembling hands clutching rosary beads, prayers invoking protection and peace. Some of the parishioners in Damascus approached me after mass and tried to ask questions about what would happen to them. *Will we be wiped out? Do other Christians think of us? Where will we go? Will the United States save us?*

The Christian minority fears that if a new government — perhaps a Muslim fundamentalist one — gets in and takes over, they will be cleared out of Syria in the same way the Armenians were driven out of Turkey or massacred in 1915.

'Alawites to the coffin, Christians to Beirut,' is one of the chants of more radical opposition members.

But Maria seemed confident for the moment. She was not going to Beirut. She sat on her roof terrace in an expansive top-floor apartment, her two small children, Perla and Roland, peeking through the windows, a Filipina maid serving tea. It could have been an ordinary day of peacetime – except that, earlier that day, there had been another car bomb.

Maria was tall, blonde, multilingual. Her husband was in the contracting business. She was someone who had bene-fited from the regime, even if she said she has felt as if she was in a minority, even if she said that while she was studying she was passed over in favour of Alawite students despite her better grades.

She was pro-government, but she wanted change. Just not yet, she said. 'We're not ready.'

She also refused to believe that the government had tortured, maimed and killed civilians. When I listed the atrocities one by one she stopped me, putting down her cup of tea. There was an angelic smile on her face.

'Do you think our president could put down his own people?' she asked me incredulously. 'Gas his own people? Kill his own people? This is the work of foreign fighters. They want to change our culture.'

Earlier in the week, I had gone to a private Saturday night piano and violin concert where the director of the opera house performed Bach, Gluck and Beethoven. She wore an elegant long dress, and the concert was held in Art House, a boutique hotel built on the site of an old mill that has water streaming over glass panels in parts of the floor.

It would not have been out of place in the Hamptons or Newport. The audience was a mix of women in spiked heels and strapless black evening gowns and bohemian men in sandals and chinos, sitting with their well-behaved children.

When everyone was seated, we were asked to stand and pay homage to the 'war dead' with a minute of silence. Everyone, even the children, remained quiet and pensive. Afterwards, the director and the pianist received a standing ovation. Then everyone in the audience filed out to an open-air restaurant and began sipping the chilled champagne that was served. I overheard several people talking in hushed voices about what had happened around the city that day: explosions and intense fighting near the suburbs.

'A toast to the symphony,' said one man, holding his glass of champagne aloft. Then he paused.

'And another toast that we will live through the next few years.'

It is easy to be cynical towards your government when they send you to fight a war and you come back with one leg and other parts of your body removed.

One scalding summer morning, a Saturday in June 2012, I drove to Barzeh, which is a toehold of the opposition inside Damascus. In Barzeh, there are frequent protests, and the government soldiers respond with arrests, shootings and killings. But Barzeh is also where the government-run Tishreen military hospital cares for wounded soldiers and takes care of the dead.

That June morning, there was a funeral for soldiers who had been killed fighting for Assad. I broke away from the hospital minder — a woman in her forties wearing high heels and a military uniform — assigned to follow me and make sure that

I was seeing what they wanted me to see, and managed to find the room where they were preparing the dead. No one noticed me as soldiers and hospital staff loaded the mangled bodies – disfigured and broken by car bombs, IEDs, bullets and shrapnel – into simple wooden coffins. They were then secured with nails before being draped with Syrian flags.

Then there was a march with the living soldiers carrying the coffins of the dead, to the strains of a gloomy marching band, into a courtyard, where families and members of their regiment waited. There were sisters, wives, mothers, brothers, children, fiancées and friends, all of their faces streaked with tears.

Soon enough, I thought, those who watch Syria closely will privately acknowledge that Assad is winning, his forces backed by Hezbollah, stronger and more determined to fight and win; his other backers of Russia and China and Iran more convincing than the opposition's backers of Qatar and Turkey (and to some extent, though not completely, the US, Britain and France).

But for today, I thought, this funeral of so many men, killed in a single day, is an acute reminder of how hard Assad's forces are getting hit by the opposition. And how brutal war is, and how it comes down to the basics – that politicians argue but soldiers fight. And soldiers are always someone's child, and that child is getting hurt. That child is getting killed.

I met an official in his office – he wouldn't give his name – but he was friendly and made me coffee. After he politely set down the sugar bowl and handed me a spoon, he pulled out a manila file and said that 105 government soldiers were dying every week. This was based on the figures of the men

he admitted to his hospital and the reports of others. He said
he had been told to keep it quiet, that the number would be
bad for morale, bad for the fighters, bad for the mothers who
had to send their sons off to war.

We sat for a while in the quiet of his office drinking the
coffee. At last, he said: 'No one likes to count the dead.'

Upstairs, on the seventh floor of the hospital, was someone's
son who had been sent to war: Firis. He was thirty years old,
a major, very handsome with long dark hair and sombre eyes.
He lay under a sheet, and I could not see at first that his right
leg and right arm were missing. He sat up when he saw me,
smiled, and with his only hand, reached out to take mine.
There was no self-pity in his demeanour. He motioned for
me to sit and he began, carefully, to tell his story.

At the end of May, Firis Jabr was in a battle in Homs. On
an afternoon of which he remembers every detail – the position of the clouds in the sky, the feel of the warm air on his
cheek – he was ambushed. Shot, he lay in a ditch bleeding
profusely and says that the men who shot him at close range
were not Syrians, but 'foreign fighters: Libyans, Lebanese,
Yemeni'.

'Are you sure they were foreign?'

'They were not Syrian. I promise – they were not
Syrian.' He said he heard their accents, that their Arabic
was not the Arabic he knew. 'They looked different, they
fought differently – I swear to you, another Syrian would
not kill his brother Syrian.'

Firis is an Alawite, but he says he is not particularly religious one way or the other. His fiancée stood near the bed

while we talked, anxiously shifting her weight from foot to foot. Firis, without a leg and an arm, spoke to me for more than an hour, and kept a smile on his face. 'I am not going to be full of pity,' he said.

'Even for war that might not have had to happen?' I asked.

He slumped back slightly on the bed. 'I was fighting for my country!'

He introduced me to his mother – 'Mama', he called her – and she made us coffee from a small hotplate in the corner of the room. She served delicate, rosewater-scented Arabic pastries with pistachios. She told me that she was a widow and that Firis was her eldest son. She was in tears as her son re-told the story of the day he was injured; her son was not. She said quietly that she did not see him as a soldier; she saw him as a small boy, playing football, walking to school with his friends – the child she carried, that she bore.

Firis said he wasn't really political, but he believed in Assad and he would continue to fight, as soon as he was fitted with his prosthetics. He said they were capable of making extraordinary false limbs – he talked about athletes who were able to run using artificial legs.

'You'll go back to the front line with an artificial leg, and an artificial arm?'

'I'm an officer – I will go wherever they send me, but yes, I would go back to the front. I would fight again.'

Firis turned and gave Mama, who had flinched when he talked about going back to fight, a bright smile.

'Don't cry,' he told her, as she turned her face to the wall. He tried to lift himself up with the side that no longer had a leg or an arm. To me he said, 'You must not pity me. I have two loves. My fiancée and Syria.'

When I left, Firis was being taken away for an examination; his mother was still looking towards the wall, the dish of uneaten pastries balanced on her lap.

4

Homs – Thursday 8 March 2012

When my son was born, shortly after the American occupation of Iraq, I was unable to cut his nails. It was a visceral, rather than rational, reaction. I would pick up the tiny baby scissors, look at his translucent fingers – clean and pink as seashells – and feel as though I would retch.

One night, in the hour before daylight, that hour when the subconscious mind allows the source of such neurosis to become clear, I suddenly understood my inability to perform such a straightforward task. I had a vision of an Iraqi man I once knew who had no fingernails.

In the dying days of the Saddam regime, pre-April 2003, I had an office inside the Ministry of Information for several months. It was a sinister, paranoid place. After a while, I fell into the bubble of that world and became paranoid myself. Staying inside the country required a special visa: one had to prostrate oneself before the Saddam officials to receive it. Journalists begged, bribed and pleaded to stay inside the country to report, offering the ministers live goats they could kill and eat for holiday meals as well as money, food, expensive wine and pharmaceutical products from the West (such as Regaine, to stop hair loss), which sanctions did not allow.

But staying inside Iraq came at a high cost. Even with visas, we were followed and videotaped. Our phones were tapped. We all knew that our hotel rooms were equipped with hidden cameras. I dressed and undressed in the darkened bathroom.

And we were surrounded by the remnants, the ghosts of Saddam's brutal regime: the terrified, the stunted, the families of the disappeared, the survivors of brutal torture.

One of these was the man with no fingernails. Every Monday morning, he arrived in my office and stretched out his hands, utterly un-selfconscious that in place of nails were bloody, raw beds of flesh. He had come for his weekly *bakhsheesh* – his bribe. His job was to get the money to seal my satellite phone so I could not use it unless the Ministry watched me. Once you paid, you would receive a seal – which only he could break – allowing you to use it. It was a backwards, futile system, of course, but everything about how Saddam operated in those days was pointless.

Every time the man arrived and I looked at his spread hands, I immediately felt a wave of panic that quickly turned to nausea. And yet, I could not take my eyes off the place where his fingernails had been ripped off. Questions that I could not ask him raced through my mind. What had he done to deserve such agony? Was he an informer? Had he tried to escape Iraq and been caught? Was he part of the secret network attempting to overthrow the dictator? I never asked. Nor would he ever have answered. We were living in a republic of fear. He became one of those sinister fixtures one holds in one's mind for ever, hovering on the fringes.

The man, whose name I never knew, seemed to bear no resentment that he had been disfigured in such a public way. Because hands are one of the first things we notice about someone, every time he stretched his out, it was immediately apparent that he had done something.

Or perhaps he had done nothing at all. Perhaps it was all a horrible mistake. Such things happen all the time in dictatorships. People get locked up for years, forgotten about. Then the key opens their cell door and a jailer says, 'You can go now.' They never know why.

The day Saddam's regime fell, I went to search for the man with no fingernails to open the seal so I could use my satellite phone. In the chaos of the American troops pulling down Saddam statues, the looting, the feverish hysteria, I still thought I needed the man to open my phone. But he, like most of the regime staff, had fled. He was hiding in a hole somewhere, like Saddam.

I went back to Iraq many times after that, but I never saw the man with no fingernails again.

In the Gaza Strip, many years ago, I stood near the Mediterranean Sea beside one of the saddest men I have ever met. His trauma was so deep that if you walked behind him and suddenly tapped him on the shoulder, he jumped. He also never smiled.

He had been imprisoned in the Israeli torture centre in the Negev Desert for fifteen months and – like those African tribesmen who believe they will die if they are imprisoned, because they have no sense of the future, only of the present – he woke every day thinking it would be his last day on earth.

'Once you have been tortured,' he told me, 'you leave the human race.'

Victims of torture often recount their methods for surviving during such barbaric pain. Someone once told me that they tried to recall complicated French verbs. Another used meditation to distance their abused and battered spirit from their body.

And yet, I have never interviewed a torture victim who has come away feeling they have not been betrayed. They say it's by the person who turned them in to the police, or by their countrymen who might be the ones doing this to them, or even by God for inflicting upon them such unthinkable horror.

In Syria, however, it is not just the torture victims who feel betrayed. The cost of loyalty on all sides – even if you believe in nothing at this point, five years into the war – has been steep.

In northern Lebanon, in a town now inhabited by refugee Free Syrian Army fighters who are recovering from severe injuries, I walked up a series of dark staircases to reach the floor where the victims of torture were recovering.

It was a secret place, in a secret location. I was asked not to write the name or the address, or the names of the men. They had been shipped by road across the Syrian border to this frontier town, and they were still afraid of Assad's spies, who could kill them, bring them back to their country, or harm their families.

As I walked around the room, I passed a man who had recently had twenty-nine bullets removed from his body. 'They just kept shooting me as though I were a piece of paper,' he said.

Then I met a paralysed man strapped to a board who was playing with a child – an orphan. The man had been badly beaten with a club by the Assad security forces and had been left with a fractured spinal cord. He lay on the board, joking with the small child, and repeated that he was exposed to the same mantra that Nada and others had been subjected to, over and over: 'Every time they hit me,' he said, 'they screamed at me, "You want freedom! Okay, take this! Here is your great freedom!"'

Next, I met a man whom I will refer to as Hussein, a student of human rights law. He was tall, thin and bearded, and had – as expected – a broken, desolate expression, which reminded me of my Gaza friend, and his words about being exiled from the human race.

Hussein was only twenty-four years old and dressed in baggy dark trousers and a T-shirt; he had a shy, but gentle demeanour. He kept trying to give me packs of Winston cigarettes, but I kept refusing, and it became a kind of farce – he kept insisting, gently, that he must give me a gift. I kept saying that I do not smoke. He would push the cigarettes across the bed sheets, where he was lying. Eventually, I took them. When I did, I saw that there were cigarette burns on his hands and arms.

On another bed, pushed against a wall, a fourteen-year-old boy sat listening. When I suggested that he leave the room for the duration of the interview, which I knew was going to be grisly and detailed, the boy explained to me earnestly that his father was killed in front of him, so he could take whatever else was about to come. 'You can speak freely,' he said.

Hussein was Sunni and religious, but he still shook my hand – which surprised me – and got off his bed, limping, to fetch me a chair. He told me that he came from an educated family; his father was a civil servant, his brothers are all university educated.

Then, without words, he began to tell his story. Slowly, he removed his T-shirt. A scar, thick and angry, began under his mid-breastbone and swam down to the proximity of his groin. He sighed, lit a cigarette, and started to talk in a low voice.

Hussein came from Baba Amr, the shattered and symbolic district in the centre of Homs. Homs is by now iconic – it is Syria's third-largest city and was under siege from May 2011 until May 2014. As of this writing – though this might change – it is under Syrian government control. But when Syrian government troops and paramilitary units initially overran Baba Amr in the spring of 2011, in the early days of the uprising against the government of Bashar al-Assad, the fighting was bitter, fierce and dirty.

Homs's population reflects Syria's general religious diversity and it is home to a community of Sunnis, Shiites, Alawites and Christians who lived side by side, only to find that – in the collapse of the police state – any sense of common purpose had dissolved.

Civil war came early to Homs, and it was fought in an urban and strategic way – one street, one building, one apartment at a time. The battle was like a seesaw: the opposition would gain ground, and then the government would take it back.

Hussein said he was never a fighter. He admitted that he was one of the organizers of the initially peaceful demonstrations that sprang up. At that time, the protests were headed by renowned Homs figures such as the Syrian television actress Fadwa Suleiman, an Alawite of the same faith as the Assad clan. That was when the demonstrations were still about slogans, marching, and chanting, as a weapon against Assad – not guns.

When the demonstrations took on a more violent nature, some of the peaceful demonstrators – like Suleiman, who now lives in France – left, disgusted by the violence. Others decided to stay and take up arms, forming the Free Syrian Army (FSA). Composed largely of disgruntled officers from Assad's forces, plus a cadre of untrained, young and inexperienced fighters, they were bound by a desire to live in a democratic country that was not governed by one family for forty years.

Hussein said he never was a member of the FSA; he swore that his allegiance to the opposition was always political and, in his case, not military. His inspiration came from the Arab Spring: watching the people of Tunisia, Libya and Egypt rise up gave him and his friends a sense of hope.

'It was about freedom and rights at first,' he said, and paused. 'Then came the bullets.'

Going back into memory is difficult even for those of us who have not withstood war or torture. Going back into war memories, or memories of physical pain and deprivation, requires a kind of iron strength. What Hussein remembered most was the physical pain, the primal sensations: cold, hunger, thirst.

That first winter in Homs was cold. Food was hard to find. Water was cut, and so was electricity. Rooms were lit by candlelight. Hussein continued:

Assad's forces launched a full assault starting at the end of February 2012. They were trying to take back our neighbourhood, Baba Amr. But the fighting and shelling had started getting really bad even in the beginning of February. By the middle of the month, people were exhausted. On the last day of February, someone told my family that the regime was 'cleansing' Baba Amr of rebels, and it would be over in a few days. Meaning we would lose our land.

I remember helicopters. I remember an entire family getting shot and killed, including the five kids. The Syrian Army's 4th Armoured Division sent in tanks and infantry.

The Free Syrian Army, the Farouq Brigades, were running away because they were afraid. People had said that they would defend Baba Amr until the last man was left standing – but they were already running away. You could not blame them – they had no weapons. We stayed in the house. By March 1st, the FSA had had enough; they made a 'tactical retreat'. A neighbour came and told us that seventeen soldiers had been captured by Assad's guys and killed immediately.

We stayed inside for a week.

On March 8th, at about 7.30 p.m. – I remember the time – I heard men speaking in a foreign language. I think it was Farsi, so they were either Iranian fighters working for Assad or they were Hezbollah . . . I don't know.

I don't know. It's so hard to remember what you wish you could forget.

At first Hussein refused to open the door. He stood behind it, and tried to talk to them. 'I said, "We are civilians! We have rights!"'

But the soldiers – who he said were not wearing uniforms, meaning that they could have been paramilitaries – fired intimidating shots, and his brother finally – if reluctantly – opened the door. As he did, the fighters shot the teenager through the chest at close range; the force of the bullet threw him against a far wall where he fell, dying. Hussein could do nothing.

They tore into the house like a swarm of bees. Hussein thinks there were about thirty of them. They immediately shot Hussein in the shoulder and hand to disable him. He was shocked, but he remembered the excruciating pain. He held up his deformed fingers, and touched the angry red circle on his shoulder blade. Once he was shot, the impact of the bullet made Hussein reel backwards, and he ended up lying next to his dying brother, looking him straight in the eye.

'I was watching the life go out of him,' he said quietly.

The men then picked him and his brother up by their hands and feet, and carried them – along with several dozen men from the neighbourhood – into a truck, throwing them inside, one on top of the other. They said they were going to use them as human shields. Some of the men in the truck were already dead; many were badly beaten and lay groaning in agony. Some were shot, others looked as if they had been beaten with clubs or rods.

'One guard pulled a man up by his ear and said, "Say Bashar al-Assad is your God." The man replied "I have no God but God," and the guard shot him and tossed him in the pile of bodies. The guard looked up at the others, defiantly. "Assad is your God!"'

Hussein was bleeding, but his brother was closer to death. They took the men in the truck to a military hospital, but not to treat them. Hussein knew what the hospital was – a place of torture, not a place of healing. The minute they closed the doors, the men who had kidnapped them began to brutally beat Hussein with sticks made of plastic and wood.

Hussein's brother was tossed in an underground room that served as a morgue. He died alone, Hussein reckons, quietly suffocating or drowning in his own blood. This was the same room in which, from then on, Hussein was thrown every night to sleep after he was tortured: on top of the dead bodies.

But he never slept, of course, lying on top of mostly corpses. Some of them were not yet dead. Hussein described how he would lie awake, listening to people breathing their last breaths. One night they tossed him on top of a body and when he turned his head, he saw his dead brother.

On his first day in captivity, Hussein's torturers, who were Syrians, introduced themselves as doctors. There were about four of them, and together they brought him into a room that appeared to be used for operations.

'Are you a fighter?'

'No, I'm a student.'

'Are you a fighter?'

He insisted: 'I'm a student. A law student.'

They held his penis and took a blade and said, 'OK, cut it off.'

They pressed the blade into his flesh, enough to draw blood; they then began leaning painfully on his bladder, forcing him to urinate.

'Why do you want to kill me?' Hussein asked, terrified and in pain.

'Because your people are killing us,' he was told.

Then they electrocuted him. This went on for three days. Beatings, burnings, cuttings. Then, again, beatings, burnings, cuttings. The worst, he says, was 'the cutting'.

'They came for me. I lay down on a table and closed my eyes. I saw them cut my gut with a scalpel. I felt nothing because I think I was still in shock. Then they lifted something out of my body – I felt pulling. It was my intestine. They stretched it. They held it in their hands and laid it on the outside of my body. They made jokes about how much the rebels ate, how much food was inside my intestines. Then they sewed me back up, but in a rough way so that there was skin and blood everywhere.'

Hussein told me his stomach was 'open' for two days before they properly stitched the wound closed.

The next day the torturers – who must have had medical knowledge – punctured Hussein's lung. They took a long plastic tube and cut an incision that runs from under his nipple to the middle of his back. They inserted what he described as a small plastic suction tube.

'I felt the air go out of my lung,' he said quietly. 'My right lung had collapsed. I could not breathe.'*

But of all the physical misery he suffered, he said the worst for him was the psychological torture – the feeling that he would never get justice, that he was being punished for something that he did not do. Because Hussein was a student of human rights law, he said he felt, above all, betrayed.

'By whom?' I asked.

By Syria, by Syrians, by his government. By his own people, who brought violence to what had started, in March 2011, as a peaceful protest for democracy.

'We have broken our country,' he said.

On and off during the days Hussein was tortured, he was hung upside down, sometimes for up to five hours. The story of his rescue is so unlikely it is almost unbelievable, and yet I met him, alive, broken but healing, in a hospital ward in northern Lebanon, several months after the event.

---

* I believe Hussein's story entirely. But I am a journalist, and the need to be objective meant that I wanted to check this story from all sides. I asked a Syrian surgeon now living in the United States (originally from Damascus, Christian Orthodox) to read this section. He did so, and he questioned the medical credibility of this account, suggesting it might have been a procedure undertaken to cure the interviewee, but without anesthetic (which is an unfortunate necessity in a war-torn country lacking basic resources). He believes it to be 'technically impossible', at least to the extent described above, but agrees the other torture methods are well documented and accurately described. However, the doctor has not lived inside Syria for some time and was not altogether familiar with the torture used under the Assad regime. This account was also checked with researchers at Human Rights Watch who had worked extensively inside Syria, and who found that, unfortunately, it could be entirely credible.

He went back in his head to those days of torture. He told me how he was 'used as a punching bag by nearly everyone that walked by as a way of having fun'. On the fifth day, when it was quiet, a doctor suddenly knelt before him.

'I am on the side of President Assad, a pro-regime doctor,' he said quietly to Hussein. 'My job is to make sure that you are still alive and can sustain more torture. But I can't watch this any more.' The doctor touched Hussein's wrist, taking his pulse.

'Your heart has technically stopped twice, once for ten seconds and once for fifteen.' The doctor leaned forward and opened a notebook. He did not look in Hussein's eyes.

'I am going to close your file and write that on the second attempt to revive you, I failed. Do you understand what I am saying? You are dead.'

He repeated it slowly. 'Do you understand what I am saying? *You are dead*. The records show that you died.'

As the doctor walked away, he said, 'If Allah intends you to live, you will find a way to get out of here.' The doctor looked at Hussein for a long moment, finally met his eyes, then was gone.

It took several minutes for Hussein to understand what the doctor meant. But the doctor ordered Hussein to be taken down from his ropes; someone lifted him, and then he was tossed back into the morgue room.

After an hour amongst the dead, in pain so brutal that he could think of nothing but the blood pumping through his ears, a female nurse came into the room.

She leaned down and whispered to Hussein that she had been paid by the Free Syrian Army to bring out any men who were still alive in this room. She told him to follow her instructions carefully: she would give him a Syrian government uniform, and a number, which he must memorize. She made him say it twice.

'Do you understand?' she said quietly. 'You have to do exactly as I say if you want to live.'

Hussein mumbled that he could stand no more, so she lifted his shirt and gave him an injection of painkiller. Then, she gently lifted him up from the bodies, and helped him put on the uniform of a government soldier.

'Hurry,' she said.

With his arm around the nurse for support, they walked out of the courtyard of the military hospital. It took twenty minutes to walk only a few feet; but later Hussein said it felt like days, walking out of that darkness. A guard asked him for his serial number. He gave the number the nurse had rehearsed with him while she nervously looked on.

On the other side of the gate, a car was waiting. He got in. It was someone sent by the Free Syrian Army. They opened the door and the nurse helped him in and turned away, without looking back. He never saw her again.

'Will anyone be jailed for what they did?' he asked. 'Will they get punished?'

I thought about it, thought about the war criminals in Bosnia, in Sierra Leone, in other wars, still at large.

I told him that I didn't know.

5

Darayya – Saturday 25 August 2012

The mechanic searched for his family for three days. He combed through destroyed buildings, checked under piles of rubble. He listened for sounds of someone calling out for help, someone who might be buried. He listened for anything. He listened for the voice of his father.

Before the war, he fixed cars. Now the sight in his right eye was gone, lost during the battle in Darayya – he thought the shrapnel that lodged in his eye came either from a helicopter bomb or possibly from a grenade. He wasn't sure. Blinded in one eye, he moved through the rubble like a ghost.

'Baba!' he called out until his voice grew hoarse.

He kept searching at night, even when it was too dangerous to be on the broken streets. There weren't many people left in Darayya, and he was afraid of the ones who were.

On the third day of searching, he found his father's body, on a farm on a road leading out of town. It was only luck that led him to take that road, and he had begun to feel that the searching was in vain. The old man was lying in the farmhouse kitchen, and there were three other bodies, beginning to decay.

They were boys, between the ages of sixteen and twenty. He closed their eyes and went back to find a car he could use to bring their bodies back to town.

He was grief-stricken, when telling me this story.

'Can you tell me why they would kill an old man?' he asked, bent over crying. 'An old man? He can't fight any more.'

The dead man's son lit a cigarette. He searched carefully for his words. 'This is not my Syria. When I see the sorrow that happens in our towns, all I think is – this is not my Syria.'

The people I later met spoke of the killing sprees that had happened on some of the hottest days of the year in the poor Sunni community of Darayya. They remembered 'intense shelling from helicopters with mounted machine-guns', 'mortars from a government military airport near the Mezzeh neighbourhood', and 'snipers in buildings' north of the city.

They spoke of soldiers moving from house to house, of informers pointing out where the activists lived; they spoke of bodies lying in the street; of groups of civilians hiding underground only to be found, lined up and summarily executed. The UK's Foreign Office Minister for the Middle East, Alistair Burt, called it 'an atrocity of a new scale, requiring unequivocal condemnation from the international community'.

Darayya, a suburb seven kilometres south of Damascus, was once known for its handmade wooden furniture. It also featured in another version of the St Paul legend. Darayya is allegedly the place where Saul had a vision of God, and became a believer. From Darayya, the enlightened man began the journey to Damascus.

But there was no miraculous vision here in August 2012, when more than 300 people, including women and children, were killed – the town was 'cleansed'.

I went there a few days after it happened. I was driven by a Sunni resident, Maryam, and we passed easily through the government military checkpoints manned by young soldiers with stubble, holding Kalashnikovs. I wore a white headscarf like Maryam, and dark sunglasses – my face was hardly visible. The soldiers, thinking we were both locals, casually waved us through. As we drove through the last checkpoint, Maryam told me about one of Darayya's most famous heroes: a twenty-six-year-old named Ghaith Matar.

Matar was a protester, but he wanted 'nothing but peace', Maryam said. He used to bring government soldiers Damascus roses and bottled water during demonstrations. 'That was before the demonstrators got met by bullets,' she said.

Matar was killed in September 2011, one year before the alleged Darayya massacre, leaving behind a twenty-year-old pregnant widow. There are rumours that he was tortured before being killed – that his throat was cut out.

The killings in Darayya came eighteen months into the war. If the figures for the dead were as high as people told us, if the civilians were really murdered in basements and shelters, laid out in the courtyard of the Abu Suleiman al-Darani Mosque, or dumped in the cemetery in the centre of town – it would be the single largest atrocity of the Syrian war.

Maryam's family came from Darayya, but they had been at their holiday home near the coast when the massacre took place between 23 and 25 August. 'It's a good thing Mama wanted to go down to the sea,' she said, taking in the destruction – the bombed-out tailor's and greengrocer's shops, the blocks of flats with their top floors blown off, the rank trash piles on corners, uncollected. There was the unmistakable smell of rotting corpses inside houses.

It was clear, despite her sangfroid, that Maryam was shocked. She had not yet decided if she supported the government or the rebels. She wanted to see for herself what had happened. She said, 'I am an open-minded woman.' Three months earlier, during the Houla massacre,[4] Maryam told me adamantly that she did not believe the reports that hundreds were dead.

Now, the reports were saying as many as 500 people were killed in Darayya, a town where her family had had an apartment for years, where she bought pine-scented chairs, a chest of drawers that she described to me in great detail: 'The craftsmanship, you cannot believe . . .'

As we drove, she pointed out where things once were before they got levelled: 'See, there was the house of the doctor . . . that was the school . . . oh no, that was where my auntie had a shop . . .' In the ashen aftermath of war, it is impossible to imagine what Darayya looked like before, or what really happened here.

To me, it looked as if it had been bombed first from the air, then house-to-house operations must have been conducted. People began to gather around us when we got out of the car – they wanted someone to hear their stories. They were shouting. They wanted to be witnesses. Some said men and boys were killed at close range with guns; others said knives were used.

'The problem is now there is no food, no water, no electricity,' J., the father of one family, told me.

J. had let his two children go outside to play and they were climbing up and down in the rubble, using it as a bridge, pretending to build small houses.

J. told me to go and talk to his smallest daughter. 'There's nothing to do, no one to play with,' said six-year-old Rauda. 'My friends left when the bombing started. I stayed close to my mother and held her. But she said we were not leaving.'

The government reports in the aftermath, and amidst the international condemnation, were that there was no massacre in Darayya. Instead, it was a 'prisoner exchange' gone wrong. The British reporter Robert Fisk, who has worked in the region for many years, accompanied Syrian Army troops into town. Fisk wrote in the *Independent* on 29 August 2012:

But the men and women to whom we could talk, two of whom had lost their loved ones on Daraya's day of infamy four days ago, told a story quite different from the popular version that has gone round the world: theirs was a tale of hostage-taking by the Free Syrian Army and desperate prisoner-exchange negotiations between the armed opponents of the regime and the Syrian army, before Bashar al-Assad's government decided to storm into the town and seize it back from rebel control.

Officially, no word of such talks between sworn enemies has leaked out. But senior Syrian officers spoke to the Independent about how they had 'exhausted all possibilities of reconciliation' with those holding the town, while citizens of Daraya told us that there had been an attempt by both sides to arrange a swap of civilians and off-duty soldiers in the town – apparently kidnapped by rebels because of their family connections with the government army – with prisoners in the army's custody. When these talks broke down, the army advanced into Daraya, only six miles from the centre of Damascus.

Fisk interviewed two people who claimed to have seen dead people on the streets even before the Syrian Army entered the town.

One woman who gave her name as Leena said . . . [she] saw at least ten male bodies lying on the road near her home. 'We carried on driving past, we did not dare to stop, we just saw these bodies in the street.' She said Syrian troops had not yet entered Daraya.

Another man said that although he had not seen the dead in the graveyard, he believed that most were related to the government army and included several off-duty conscripts. 'One of the dead was a postman – they included him because he was a government worker,' the man said.

Fisk concluded: 'If these stories are true, then the armed men . . . were armed insurgents rather than Syrian troops.'[5]

But, to be fair, Fisk was accompanying government troops and perhaps the two people he interviewed told him what the soldiers around him wanted to hear (or they were frightened). The people I saw said that the government tanks had rolled right down the centre of town, destroying everything in sight, crushing the street lights, the houses, even the graveyard walls. Then the killing started.

There seemed to be no window left in town that was not shattered. In the middle of some buildings that were crushed like accordions, I saw a lone cyclist with a cardboard box of tinned groceries strapped to a rack over his back wheel. He said he was trying to find his home.

In another building, I found a man hiding in the aftermath of the killing. He had just been released after six months in prison.

Rashid had been arrested in December 2011, although he said he was not a member of the Free Syrian Army.

'They told me that I was one of the organizers of the strikes,' he said.

He was taken to Jawiya Air Force Prison near the Mezzeh neighbourhood, stripped of his clothes, made to stand outside in freezing temperatures and doused with cold water. He was then beaten with sticks and fists.

'I stayed there for five hours, freezing, my hands tied behind my back, and they kept asking if I was organizing strikes.'

He was then hung with his hands behind his back so that his shoulders were pulled out of their sockets. He kicks off his dusty sandals to show the bottoms of his feet and the angry, red scars that reveal where he had been whipped and beaten. 'The electrocution was the easiest of it.'

At night he was kept in a four- by five-metre room that he says housed 150 men. They all had to stand and make one place for sleeping, in which they took turns lying down. He stayed six months in jail.

'The problem is they forget about you,' he said. 'Then one day, they just came and said, okay, it was a mistake, you can go.' Human Rights organizations have documented that there are – as of this writing – nearly 38,000 Syrians now being held in detention, often without their families knowing their whereabouts or why they were taken.

Rashid describes the attack on Darayya, which took place the Saturday before, the fourth day of the Eid holiday.

'The shelling started at 7.30 a.m. There is no sound more frightening than rockets,' he said.

Sunday continued with more shooting and shelling, and then finally, on Monday, he said the army arrived. Most people hid in basements. Some were pulled out and executed outside; according to witnesses, others were sprayed with machine-gun fire.

'We had some informers [the word in Arabic is *awhyny*] who pointed out where Opposition people were,' he said. 'They let the women run away but they shot the men one by one. In some cases, they went into the basement and killed old men and children – just because they were boys.'

Another woman who was cooking for victims and taking food to the mosque, Umm Hussein, was hurrying along during the bombardment with her young daughter and twenty-year-old son. A truck went by with soldiers shouting: 'With our life, with our blood, we will fight for Assad!'

Umm Hussein and her children did not make it in time: they were stopped and while she and her daughter were spared, her son was shot. She says his body was taken out of town; there are rumours that some victims are being moved to secondary graves, which was also the case with the Srebrenica massacre in Bosnia in 1995.

But some people I meet say that the regime soldiers fed them and provided medical attention to the wounded. 'They gave us bread,' one man says. 'Not all of them were monsters.'

In the initial days after the chaos, no one knew who was dead or alive. The VDC (Centre for Documentation of Violations) put the figure at somewhere around 380. The Syrian opposition put it in the thousands.

The mounds of freshly dug, moist earth in the cemetery in the middle of town looked as if they harbour at least several hundred dead. One woman came every day to scan a list posted outside the graveyard; she was looking for her sons, who are missing: 'We are still searching houses and abandoned ruins trying to find them.' She says that everyone waits for the hour when the gravedigger arrives, because then there will be new bodies to identify.

After a while, Maryam and I went to look for the gravedigger to see if he could give us a more accurate count of the dead. There was a tightly packed crowd of people who were reading a sign put up by desperate families – a list of the missing. They parted and let us through to look at the sign.

That's where I met the mechanic. It was there, looking over the list, that he told me: 'Syrians cannot do this to other Syrians.'

Many of the bodies were discovered on the fifth day, when Human Rights Watch obtained satellite images of the battle. Initially, they were not clear if the killing was committed by government forces, or whether Shabiha militia carried out the assassinations after the town was shelled and bombed by helicopters: 'What we don't know yet is who did the dirty work, the executions – whether it was men in uniform or Shabiha,' Ole Solvang, from HRW, told me a few weeks after the battle. 'We're still talking to people.'

'I think whoever did it,' Maryam told me solemnly, 'they were trying to teach Darayya a lesson.'

But why? Why teach a town a lesson? And who were they? One Syrian journalist later told me that Iranian militias were also working alongside the Syrian Army.[6]

Darayya was long regarded as a bastion of opposition and a base for the Free Syrian Army. Eventually, 3,000 FSA fighters made Darayya their stronghold, as it was strategically situated on the edge of the military airport at Mezzeh, a town being used for air strikes against rebel-held areas. Both rebels and local residents reported that opposition forces conducted mortar and rocket strikes against the base from Darayya. Also, a few days before the government attack, the rebels claimed to have killed thirty soldiers when they attacked a military checkpoint outside the town.[7]

But there are some reports that the FSA began withdrawing from their holding positions at least two days before, to spare the town from being pummelled.

Not long before the massacre, there was a week of gruesome discoveries of the bodies of people summarily executed by regime forces, which began turning up in Damascus suburbs, such as Douma. In the northeast area of that city, sixteen men were found executed, allegedly by regime forces.

Shortly after, in an extraordinary act of indecency, a pro-regime television journalist, Micheline Azaz, entered the town and filmed a fourteen-minute piece on camera, largely interviewing victims who needed medical care. She interrogated them before they were removed by emergency services, when they were still in immense pain and shock, demanding to know if 'terrorists' had done this.

Azaz, who worked for the Syrian channel Addounia, was shown interviewing victims against a backdrop of classical music. The cameraman first filmed close-ups of several corpses stretched out on the ground or in cars.

'As usual, by the time we arrive at the scene,' Azaz said breathlessly, 'the terrorists have already done what they do best: committed criminal acts, murdered people . . . and all in the name of freedom.'

She then approached an elderly woman who appeared to be in agony, waiting for medical help. Azaz extended the microphone with perfectly manicured hands and demanded to know who was responsible.

Then she found a small child, about five years old, in a car sitting next to a lifeless body.

'Who is that?' Azaz asked the child.

'My mother,' replied the girl.

A woman named Reem, who lived in Darayya, was there when Azaz did her broadcast. 'It was horrific,' she said. 'She was a vulture. She went through the crowds talking to the wounded as though she was floating on water, as though there was not this scene of hell in front of her . . .'

For weeks, the blame went back and forth – the government blaming the FSA and other armed 'terrorists', the witnesses I spoke to blaming the government.

The day after I left Darayya – after government soldiers found me talking to people and, rather remarkably, calmly asked that I get out of town instead of arresting me – I went to see a government official.

Abeer al-Ahmad, who was the Director of Foreign Media at the Ministry of Information (MOI),[8] was in her office drinking coffee with an opened box of biscuits in front of her, and she was visibly furious. Even before I told her, she knew I had been inside Darayya – no one does anything in Syria without the secret police knowing.

'It was a prisoner exchange of terrorists gone wrong,' she insisted. 'It's always been a hideout for terrorists. It was meant to be part of a wider campaign in the southern suburbs to rid the area of the opposition forces.'

A few days later, she alerted me to a statement made by the President himself. 'The Syrian people will not allow this conspiracy to achieve its objectives,' Assad said. 'What is happening now is not only directed at Syria but the whole region. Because Syria is the cornerstone, foreign powers are targeting it so their conspiracy succeeds across the entire region.'

'So you are blaming foreign forces for Darayya?' I asked her.

'Something like that.' She made it clear the meeting was over.

The official state news agency, SANA (Syrian Arab News Agency), stated, 'Our heroic armed forces cleansed Darayya from remnants of armed terrorist groups who committed crimes against the sons of the town.' It accused the 'terrorists' of carrying out their own massacre.

The Syrian journalist I spoke to earlier remembered this:

There was a story of a little girl who bribed a Syrian soldier as she escaped her family's massacre running. She told him 'I have 500 Syrian pounds on me, take them and don't kill me.'

He took them and didn't kill her. Another little girl begged one of the soldiers as they were ready to massacre her whole family, that she has savings, that she will give it all to the soldier. She was begging – in return that they do not kill her eleven-month-old brother. They shot away . . . but she and her brother did survive.[9]

When last I checked with them, Human Rights Watch said there was no indication of Free Syrian Army atrocities. 'It was either government or pro-government forces behind the executions,' the researcher told me.

But I still remember what I witnessed those days.

When we left the town, crossing through the check-points, Maryam suddenly cried out: 'Look! They destroyed our mosque!' Then she grew silent, pensive, grave. I didn't hear her say another word until she dropped by my hotel later that night. There she told me that 'even the French during the occupation did not destroy mosques when people took refuge in holy places'. She was disturbed. She raised her voice: 'This is a crime against God . . . and Alawites believe in God as well as Sunnis.' She was close to tears as she turned to me, saying later that it was in this moment that she truly realized that people were certainly killing each other.

'Why?'

Maryam shrugged. 'No reason. I can't answer.'

One side says this, the other says that. The town also shifted hands several times. From August 2012, government forces kept the town until November 2012, when another battle of Darayya played out. First the rebels pushed back, then, according to *Al Watan* newspaper – which is close to the government – on 20 December, after thirty days of siege, the army penetrated the last areas of the city centre that the rebels held. *Al Watan* claimed most of the fighters were foreigners, playing into the narrative that jihadis were taking over Syria. The next day they launched a massive attack against the city, but rebels reported they met a strong resistance from Darayya. The government remained in control and AFP reported that in August Assad visited the 'ex-rebel bastion', now mainly under government control, his first known visit outside the capital since March 2012.

By December 2013, government forces were hitting the town with barrel bombs. From 25 to 31 January 2014, as United Nations representatives met with opposition and government officials in Switzerland for the Geneva II 'talks', the regime continued to bomb Darayya mercilessly.[10]

Reporters asked Walid Muallem, the Syrian Foreign Minister, at the Geneva talks why his government continued to use barrel bombs. Muallem replied: 'I want to give you a simple response. Do you want [us] to defend our people by sending SMS messages?'

The film mentioned in note 10, made by a local cameraman, opens with the words: 'Once upon a time: a few days ago. In a land far, far away: Syria.'

By April 2014, government reporters claimed Darayya was mainly being fought for by foreign rebels. The grey plumes of dusty smoke from the bombs could be seen from the highway. When the smoke cleared, there was nothing left behind but skeletons of buildings, of people, of what was once a town.

Maryam never went back.

My government visas were revoked a few months after I entered Darayya 'illegally'.

As of March 2015, my requests to return to Syria 'legally' on the government side of the war were met with silence, threats or excuses from the regime.

Once, a Syrian friend went to the Ministry of Information on my behalf to plead my case; she was told that if she wanted to 'save my ass from getting thrown in a Syrian jail' then she should tell me never to come back to Syria.

6

Zabadani – Saturday 8 September 2012

By the autumn of 2012, in the wake of Darayya, the evolving skirmishes in Syria had become a full-blown war. The denial that had existed a few weeks before among a certain class in Damascus, the bubble of parties, the insouciant chatter, the seductive evenings at the opera, were gone. That bubble had burst. Four men in Assad's closest circle had been assassinated, probably with the help of FSA members who had infiltrated the government. People were talking about the fall of Damascus. There was heavy fighting in other parts of Syria – in Idlib, in Aleppo, and in the suburbs not far from the capital. If Damascus fell, the country fell.

A Syrian reporter I met through friends invited me to her house, then texted me emphatically to arrive only after dark, and to take the stairs, not the lift, to avoid people seeing me.

When I arrived, the woman's face was darkened with worry. The reporter, who we will call Renda, had been famous in the 1990s. She was a well-known commentator and politically considered herself 'pro-Assad, but liberal'. 'I say what I think,' she had told me. 'I am outspoken.' She had initially taken a strong stand behind Assad and against the rebels. Now she was not so sure. She wanted to meet me to see if I would take her to Homs so that she could see the destruction for herself.

Renda quickly ushered me inside her small, modern apartment and locked the door behind her. 'I don't want to let the neighbours see you here,' she said. 'I've been getting all kinds of threatening emails for the past few days. And someone keeps calling me and hanging up when I answer.' She shrugged. 'It's the Mukhabarat. What are they going to do? They want to frighten me.'

We sat and drank green tea and she told me that she had only felt in the past two weeks that her world was spinning out of control, that a real war had come to Syria, that perhaps she had judged the opposition wrongly. She had begun to question what was happening in Homs, in Aleppo. Even Darayya, which she did not really believe . . . but …

'Only now? You only realize it now?'

Renda nodded. She clutched her hands in her lap. 'It's not my fault – who wants to see their country turning to war? You avoid it if you can, you avoid thinking about it. You don't want to believe it.' But now, she said, 2,000 people had fled the capital alone. Refugees were flooding the Turkish, Jordanian and Lebanese borders. The winter was going to be harsh. 'If Syrians go to Lebanon as refugees, the Lebanese will not welcome them entirely,' she added. 'Look at the situation of the Palestinians there.'

She had no way of knowing, but in two years' time, more than four million Syrians would be refugees, crossing the borders and fleeing to neighbouring Jordan, Iraq, Lebanon and Egypt. The luckier ones – or maybe not so lucky, as the migrant crisis in the late summer of 2015 demonstrated – got to Europe in boats, with the help of smugglers, or on foot. There would also be nine million displaced people inside Syria by 2015. By the end of the summer of 2013, Renda would also close up her small apartment and leave for Beirut, going by road with a few suitcases, planning to stay for a few weeks; but she would stay for months, then eventually – without being aware of time passing – she imagined she would be there for years.

One morning, Maryam and I had permission to go to visit her relatives in Homs, which was divided into government-held and rebel-held areas. Maryam's family were Sunnis, but they were on the government side, at least geographically, if not philosophically. We took her mother, Rosa, along with us, and put her in the front seat. I put on my white head-scarf, which matched Maryam's and Rosa's, and my big dark glasses. Rosa assured me I looked Syrian. At every check-point, Syrian government soldiers did not even bother to look in the back seat and see me, a foreigner.

'Go ahead, grandma,' they said to Rosa, and let us pass. She chastised a few of them ('what would your mother say about your bad manners?'), and when we were held at one particular checkpoint for several hours, inside Homs, she began to lecture them about their 'rudeness to adults'.

'Do you really think I want to be here, *Teta*?' he asked her incredulously. 'Do you think I want to be a soldier?' They showed us around the house they had confiscated from a Sunni family and were now living in. A few bedrooms with dirty sheets, where soldiers with muddy boots were loung-ing, sitting with a teakettle. There was no phone line to their headquarters, and they did not want to let us go. They sat talking to Rosa for hours, about their families, their holidays, their children, their schooling.

Eventually, they let us go. 'They're not bad boys,' said Rosa, who had been the wife of a successful and wealthy Damascus businessman. 'Slightly ill-brought up, but not bad boys. They are provincial, it's not their fault.'

Maryam's family, which included mainly elderly aunts and an uncle, made us an elaborate lunch of many courses. It was indulgent and embarrassed me because I knew that they were struggling to get food. 'Just be quiet and eat,' Maryam whispered, passing a plate. 'You'll insult them if you refuse, so say nothing.'

There was a sort of thick lentil soup, rice, roasted chicken, there were piles of bread, there was even tinned fruit. Everyone ate quietly as we heard shelling coming from a nearby government base. Maryam had asked me emphatically not to talk politics with her family. 'They have lived for so long under the Assad regime that they are frightened of talking to outsiders,' she said. 'So don't ask, don't put them in danger.' So we talked about classical music, the opera and the British Museum. One of her cousins had been imprisoned for years in Hama during the crackdown on the Muslim Brotherhood in the early 1980s; then he went to live in Aleppo. Maryam had briefed me beforehand not to talk about it. 'He still has nightmares from those years in prison,' she said. 'We choose not to talk about it. And since people now suspect radical jihadis are entering the country, he has to be very careful.'

One of the older aunts, Rosa's sister, a lady with a soft gentle face, got up from the table and changed into a nightdress. She said she was lying down to take a nap. Rosa picked up her coffee cup and said she would join her, in an adjoining bedroom. The two elegant, elderly ladies then left the room, before quickly running back to the table a few moments later when a particularly heavy bomb landed somewhere nearby.

'This is the background music of our lives,' the uncle said 'since we are talking about Bach at lunchtime.' The relatives did not want their neighbours to see foreigners staying with them, so as the day ended Maryam and I left Rosa, crossed town and stayed in a darkened hotel where the secret police called me to their table and questioned me at length about why I was there. I pulled out my note of permission from Damascus, but they still held me for an hour, while Maryam – who was partially deaf and so spoke louder than most people, her shrill voice rising to a high pitch when she was angry – argued with them to let me go. Eventually, they did. We slept that night to the accompaniment of heavy shelling.

The next morning, we left Rosa, who had not slept well and was irritated with the aunts over some small family matter, and headed towards Latakia, in the Alawite heartland. We wanted to see the mausoleum of Hafez al-Assad, the father of Bashar, who had been president from 1971 until his death in 2000. We passed checkpoint after checkpoint until we got closer to Qardaha, the burial site. There were stone lions everywhere; Assad means *lion* in Arabic and is the name Bashar's grandfather had adopted as a family name.

Maryam was suddenly very conscious of her white hijab. 'We are in the land of Alawites now,' she said when we stopped at a café overlooking one of the austere mountains

THE MORNING THEY CAME FOR US

surrounding Latakia. She picked up her can of Pepsi. 'I feel
uncomfortable.'

'But you're Syrian. Your family has a home nearby.'

'I don't feel Syrian here,' she said. 'This is Alawite country.'
I had never heard Maryam mention sectarian divides before,
and she gave me an abridged history of the Alawites. 'They
feel different. They *are* different.'

The Alawites are a minority religious branch of Shia
Muslims that represent about 12 per cent of the Syrian population. The core of Alawite belief differs from mainstream
Islam; for this alternative belief, the Sunni rulers of the area
had historically persecuted Alawites. But, during the period
of French rule in the interwar years, an Alawite state was
carved out in modern-day Latakia, meant to keep Alawites
safe from persecution. The French considered the Alawites
and Druze to be the only 'warlike races' in the mandate territory, for which reason the Alawites were largely recruited
into the French forces, and still compose a large section of
the modern Syrian army (indeed, this is how Hafez al-Assad
rose to power). But despite the Alawites' prominence in the
armed forces, the majority of this group worked as labourers
for Sunni landowners, a fact that had fostered the animosity
between these groups.

When the waiter came to take our order, Maryam motioned
to me to be quiet. 'It's a good thing Mama is not here,' she
muttered when the waiter went away.

At the grandiose Assad family mausoleum, the guards –
young men in sombre, well-cut blue suits – were friendly.
They were surprised to see a foreigner and served me tea
before escorting me inside to the green marble-covered

graves where Hafez and two of his sons were buried. They gave me his condensed biography – how he had been the first Alawite to go to high school, how the Alawites had been subjugated by the French before Syrian independence. As they spoke, pouring more tea, the air heavy with the scent of roses and incense, I looked at an empty corner of the mausoleum and wondered if the current president, Bashar, would soon find his place there as well.

'We may never see this again,' Maryam said as we left, passing another lion. 'If the regime crumbles, the opposition will tear this place down to the ground.' I turned around to fix it, visually, in my mind, like taking a Polaroid. In the dying days of Saddam Hussein's regime, I had done the same in Iraq. I had obtained permission from an equally restrictive Ministry of Information to drive from Basra to Mosul, visiting ancient monuments and archaeological ruins, which I knew, with a horrible sense of political foreboding, I would never again see in my lifetime.

We drove out of the village, and headed into the Jibal al-Alawiyin mountains, stopping to eat at a roadside restaurant. A river rushed below us, as the blue-eyed waiter – many Arabs of the Levant have blue eyes, but particularly Alawites – took a seat at the table with us. Talking to Maryam, he said he had moved to Latakia when he was a child. As an Alawite, he told us that he constantly felt marginalized: even as part of the minority that controlled the country.

When he left the table, Maryam said, 'He feels marginalized? Seventy-four per cent of the country is Sunni Muslims, but most of the government jobs and postings are occupied by Alawites.'

The waiter came back with bottles of mineral water.

'The Europeans don't understand us,' the waiter complained. 'Everyone takes the side of the rebels. But as Syrians – all of us – we are all losing so much.'

Two men at the next table were listening to us. They were Alawite businessmen, dressed in suits, smoking cigarettes. They were down from Damascus for work, and they were drinking *rakia*, a form of brandy made with aniseed, a drink that is also popular in Turkey and the Balkans.

'May we join you?' one asked, bringing the bottle and his glass before we answered. They wanted to know why I was in Syria, what I thought of the country, and what I was going to report. Although she was too savvy to give anything away, I could feel Maryam's discomfort. She was brave simply to be with me, to take me to Homs, to Latakia, to places that she really should not be showing a foreigner.

'Feel free to talk,' one of the men said warmly. 'We want to hear your opinion.' The waiter brought our food, but no one ate.

At first we spoke blandly, drinking *rakia*, being careful not to probe, not to ask sensitive questions. After several glasses of *rakia*, I asked them about what happened to men like Hussein, who were captured and tortured in Baba Amr.

There was visible stiffening, then a determined silence. One of the men reached for the bottle, the other lit a cigarette. The plate of lamb that the waiter had brought us, along with the roast potatoes, remained untouched.

'That does not happen,' said the one with the glass. 'It's propaganda.'

'But it does happen,' I insisted, 'on both sides.'

Maryam changed the subject rapidly and abruptly stood up. 'We need to drive back to Damascus,' she said, trying hard to smile in a friendly way. We attempted to pay the bill – the men would not let us – and left. She said nothing until we got to the car.

'They weren't lying,' she said finally. 'They really don't believe this is happening. You see Syrians simply cannot bear that we are doing this to each other. At least, civilized, educated Syrians.'

She was quiet for a long while, fiddling with the radio stations. Then she spoke. 'Once we had a common enemy – Israel. Now we are each other's enemy.'

A few days later, we went to an old summer retreat in the mountains outside of Damascus, Zabadani, where Maryam had come as a child to breathe in the fresh air. 'It was a place where you went for peaceful drives with your family, to get out of the city, to have some country food,' she said. Now the Free Syrian Army was holding the town, although it had changed hands so many times – from government forces to rebels, back to government, back to rebels – that even Maryam, whose brother was close to the FSA, was not sure who held it.

Zabadani was on an old smugglers' route from Lebanon before the war, and had been mainly populated by civilian Sunnis, but it was now full of soldiers. The al-Shabab, the guys, the rebel fighters, who were at that point said to be funded by Qatar and Saudi Arabia, had old guns, some of them from the days when their fathers took them hunting. There were no anti-tank weapons or anti-aircraft guns. They were wearing sneakers with their uniforms.

They told me that before the war, Zabadani had been one of those places where religion and ethnicity had not mattered. If it did, it was not used as a method of divisiveness.

'There was a feeling of belonging in Zabadani that the regime deprived us of,' said Mohammed, a young journalist I had met in Beirut. He was born and raised in Zabadani, but had been forced to flee at the start of the uprising because he was involved in opposition politics. 'We felt *Syrian* more than any ethnic or religious denomination.'

In a sense, one of the many tragedies of the war was the re-emergence of religious ties. Assad's regime, though a dictatorship, was at least allegedly nationalist; that is to say that nationality was stressed to be more important than one's ethnicity or religion. That is why Assad tended to find support among minority groups such as Alawites and Christians. Was it the brutal war itself, rather than the regime and Assad's policies, that destroyed the sense of Syrian unity in Zabadani?

On the day we arrived, I was told there had been fifty-two straight days of shelling. We drove from Damascus, first to the house of a farming family who lived high above the town, then the farmer loaded us into his car and we drove down to the centre of Zabadani. A small unit of men was crowded into a courtyard of an old house that had been badly shelled. They were sitting, doing the same thing that soldiers all over the world do when they are waiting for an attack, or to be attacked: they were smoking cigarettes, they were drinking tea.

So what did you do in your former life? I asked them. One was a mason, one was a truck driver, another was a teacher, another a smuggler who came from a long line of smugglers in Zabadani. 'Thirty years ago,' he said, 'everyone on the road between Damascus and Zabadani was smuggling. Levis, cigarettes, electrical things, anything.'

'Once,' the smuggler continued, realizing he had the attention of the entire courtyard, 'I got a shipment of Lacoste T-shirts, real ones, with the alligator . . .'

A burst of machine-gun fire outside the door. He stopped talking. Someone came in and told them to move. We hustled out into another building.

The hospital in Zabadani that day was a former furniture shop. It kept getting relocated because every few days the government found out where it was and shelled it. When I walked in, the doctor was stitching up the leg of a soldier in his late teens who had been hit by shrapnel. The doctor worked slowly and methodically, pulling the thread through the two sides of the wound, and talking quietly to the soldier, who did not flinch.

'After Darayya,' he said, meaning the battle in the suburb of Damascus a few weeks before, 'there's no going back. There was a time we felt maybe this was not real, maybe it was not really war – not really war.' He finished stitching and cut the thread with a small pair of scissors. 'Now I am working in a furniture store, trying to save lives. We've moved six times in the past two weeks because we keep getting hit. We're all demoralized.'

He guided me around the small back room, and introduced me to the other patients: kids who had shrapnel lodged in their flesh, another soldier with a head wound. Before I left, he insisted on giving me a medical kit, although I told him I did not need it. 'Please,' he said. 'You need it. You must take it.'

As I left, his wife ran to our car. She had brought a gift, some freshly washed pears that came from the trees that were still blooming and growing fruit throughout Zabadani.

'Pears were the symbol of Zabadani,' said the doctor. 'They used to be the sweetest thing.'

At 10 a.m. Central Europe Time on 22 February 2012, while I was in Belgrade with LR, someone in Beirut rang to tell me that the journalist Marie Colvin was dead. She had been hit by a massive explosion in Baba Amr, in Homs. I had seen her a few weeks before, talked of our boyfriends, of clothes, of work, of visions. When the phone call came, I was at the gym. I slipped into the locker room, leaned against a wall and sat stunned: how many more colleagues would die in this war?

Marie was fifty-eight. She had gone through many conflicts. She had lost an eye working in Sri Lanka, sustained a difficult recovery, then went back to work wearing an eye patch. She rarely complained. Now, edging towards sixty, with a whole new tribe of war reporters coming up in her wake, she wanted a peaceful life, one where she could write, and read, and sail boats across challenging waters. As committed as she was to telling the story – she once told me the book that changed her life was John Hersey's *Hiroshima* – she did not want to go to Homs on this particular trip; she had a bad feeling. But she was a professional, and she went, and she ended her days in a lonely street in the middle of a strange and foreign country, in the middle of a war. There was a moment when the shelling got so bad in Homs that she finally wanted to leave, but by then, it was too late. It's usually too late by the time you reach that conclusion.

I booked a flight to London immediately, and my friend LR drove me to the airport, allowing me the space to be silent. The phone kept ringing non-stop – it was as though Marie's death was a wake-up call for so many of us who did this work.

Marie died quickly, they say, but her body lay in Homs while intricate negotiations went on to bring her home. Eventually, after much negotiation, her battered body was driven to Beirut and then flown home to Long Island, where she grew up. Finally, I supposed, she was at peace. But I could not help thinking about her dying on a street in Homs. My only solace was that someone who was with her had said she died quickly. Perhaps she did not know what was coming, but I kept thinking about her last moments, waking up in the top floor of a house in Baba Amr, hearing the intense crack of shelling, running downstairs to put on her shoes to go outside, bending to tie them, getting hit by the blast. Never going home again, never saying goodbye to the people you loved, never getting to tell your last story.

After that, every time I went to Syria I was afraid. And that was a good thing. I was liberated, realizing that the normal emotion that most people felt when they went into one of the most dangerous places on earth had finally reached me. It did not particularly change the way I worked, but it slowed me down, particularly once ISIS had arrived, and once the kidnapping began.

After my second trip to Damascus with a government visa in 2012, I returned to Paris and thought often of a small child I met in Homs, with whom I had passed a gentle afternoon. At night, the sniping started and his grandmother began to cry for fear of being found with a foreigner in her house. She made me leave in the dark.

I did not blame her. She did not want to die. She did not want her home to be raided by the Mukhabarat for harbouring a foreign reporter.

The boy had been indoors for some months and he was bored: he missed his friends. He missed the life that had ended for him when the protests began.

For entertainment, he watched, over and over, the single video in the house: *Home Alone*. Like waiting on Groundhog Day, he was waiting for the end of this winter, waiting for normality to return so he could go out and play, find the school friends who months ago had been sent to Beirut or London or Paris to escape the war, and resume his school lessons.

'When will it end?' he asked earnestly. For children, there must always be a time sequence, an order, for their stability. As a mother, I know this. My son is confused by whether he sleeps at his father's apartment, or his mother's, and who is picking him up from school.

'And Wednesday is how many days away?' he always asks me. 'And Christmas is how many months? And when is summer?'

'So when is the war over?' this little boy asked me.

'Soon,' I said, knowing that I was lying. I knelt down and took his tiny face in my hands. 'I don't know when, but it will end,' I said. I kissed his cheek goodbye and lied again.

'Everything is going to be fine.'

7

Homs, Bab al-Sebaa Street –
Sunday 14 October 2012

It was early autumn in Homs, the heat was subsiding, the air was beginning to turn cool. I had come back, with a government visa, with strict orders from Abeer to 'Behave. Tell the truth. Stop telling lies about the Syrian people.'

I asked her to let me travel with the Syrian Army, and she said she would think about it – 'I'm not sure you will tell the truth about the battle we are waging,' she said suspiciously. Finally, on a weekday morning, she telephoned me before breakfast. 'You can go,' she said. 'You can see our brave boys and what the terrorists are doing to them.'

So I found myself on the other side of the city, the other side of the war. I was technically embedded with the Syrian Arab Army (SAA), the force branch of the Syrian Armed Forces, who have played the active role of 'governance' in Syria since 1946. The unit I was assigned to were trying to take out a sniper who was targeting their men inside a hollowed-out building. We had to crouch because the sniper was so close; he could see us through the windows.

I was with Rifaf, whose name in Arabic means the sound of a bird's soft fluttering wings. He was holding his Kalashnikov, waiting for the next incoming, large-calibre, automatic weapon fire. Rifaf was tense and because I was so close to him that I could see the muscles in his cheek twitching and smell the cigarettes on his breath, his tension spread to my own body. Fear has its own physiology.

We had reached Bab al-Sebaa on foot, running across abandoned boulevards and empty houses. You drive to the last possible safe area, but then vehicles must be abandoned. The army had guided me through a tangle of buildings to reach this place. We crawled through tunnels punched into the walls of buildings known as 'mouse holes'. These allowed soldiers to move from one building to the next, to breach one obstacle after another, without having to go out onto the street and expose themselves to incoming rockets and sniper fire. Other buildings were connected through alleys where buildings have collapsed, and we walked across planks, piles of shattered glass and improvised bridges leading from one building to the next.

We inched forward slowly. It took us an hour to reach the building we wanted to be in. Normally, it would probably have taken five minutes.

The Ministry of Information had sent a 'minder' along to watch me. Shaza was in her thirties, outspoken, brave, and an ardent supporter of Assad – she did not have to accompany me to the front line, but she wanted to see what it was like for the 'boys'. She had a sense of humour: 'Next time,' she panted to me as we were crawling through a hole, 'don't wear a pink headscarf. The snipers can see you.'

The men in the unit near Bab al-Sebaa were young, raw recruits, with a few older career officers. They were very tired.

Bleary-eyed with fatigue, they were still courteous, surprised to see me, curious. They were not the macho horrors I'd imagined I would meet – they were kids. The most 'macho' they got was when they would sometimes punch the air in a rush of adrenalin and chant, 'God! Syria! Syria and God!' But even that war cry seemed depleted.

As we crossed the urban landscape, the soldiers pointed out their positions. Some were alone with their weapons, on the first or second floors of buildings that were not in as vulnerable a position as ours; some were in sniper positions higher up; others were clustered in small units of four or five. 'If you are alone, it gets boring, boring, BORING,' one said.

'Do you get frightened?'

The kid who said he got bored stood up and moved back towards me. 'Only an idiot is not frightened.' Exactly on cue there was more gunfire. He picked up his gun and returned to his position.

The commander of Rifaf's unit – who did not want to give his name but called himself M. – said he wasn't sure how many rebel soldiers, then mostly Free Syrian Army (FSA), were left in Homs. Their stronghold was the Old City. There could have been anywhere from 1,500 to 2,000 of them left.

'No one knows,' M. said. They were 'reasonably adequate, sometimes good' fighters. 'They know what they are doing,' he continued. 'But we are bigger, we are more powerful, and they are trying to wear us down.'

I thought of Hussein while I was there, who was tortured in Homs by Assad's men – comrades of the men I was now with. But it was hard for me not to like Rifaf, and I wanted to listen to his specific and personal version of events. In Rifaf's eyes, it went like this: Alawites were members of a minority group who have been oppressed throughout Syria's history. They were continually trodden upon, persecuted, and are now endangered by the radicalization and jihadization of their country.

'Surely all the FSA fighters aren't fighting for Islamic jihad,' I said. 'Aren't some of them fighting for a democratic country, without Assad?'

'I'm not really a political guy,' Rifaf said, cutting the conversation short. 'I do what I am told.' When I told him about Hussein's guts being cut out of him by an Assad government soldier-doctor, he was horrified.

Like every soldier I ever met in any war, Rifaf wishes he were somewhere else, somewhere other than a cold room, bending low, waiting for a sniper to strike again. 'He's there,' Rifaf said, shifting his position to peer below a grilled window. He nodded his head towards a blasted-out building less than 300 metres away. The building – a former school – was a weapons depot. The government troops hoped to take it by day's end. He said we had hours to wait, and that the sniper had been shooting all day.

This is what war is like, I thought: waiting to conquer inch by inch, room by room, building by building, street by street, eventually neighbourhood by neighbourhood. It's tedious. So much time is spent lighting cigarettes, waiting for the next shot, the next place to aim. Taking territory back is not a blaze of gunfire: it's a methodical, protracted process.

Burst of gunfire.

The room Rifaf and his unit (his 'brothers') have turned into their 'nest' was once someone's bedroom, in a house that has long since been abandoned. That person's home is now a sniper's nest. Their clothes, their photographs, their lives have been erased.

There's more gunfire, and the sharp sound of the sniper responding. 'Hours, days maybe to take one building,' Rifaf mutters. 'This is how it goes. We get one inch, they take back one inch. They get one inch, we take it back.'

'It's like playing cat and mouse,' says another soldier, positioned in a corner not far from us.

This is how urban wars are fought: cat and mouse.

'Who's the cat, who's the mouse? You or the sniper?'

Rifaf laughed. He did not answer.

All summer long, while Hussein lay in a hospital bed, recovering from his stomach having been sliced open, the war in Homs continued: fluid, deadly and slow. It moved at an inexorable pace. The soldiers who brought me here, who clambered over piles of rubble, were waiting: for the right moment to take out the enemy soldier, for the right moment to charge the building, for the right moment to go home. Occasionally, perhaps remembering why they were there, they would sing:

With our hearts
With our souls
We fight for you, Assad!

When the Syrian government launched a new offensive in Homs at the beginning of October 2012, Rifaf and his unit were assigned this position and given a clear objective: to take the building opposite from rebel hands. This means a kind of close-quarters battle, urban warfare similar to how the siege of Sarajevo was fought, or the first Chechen war, or the battle of Beirut. The British military call it Offensive Operations in Built Up Areas – OBUA; Americans call it UO – Urban Operations.[11] It is taxing on ordnance, ammunition, supplies and manpower. But it is necessary in cities – the only way to fight. Rifaf and his unit were struggling to maintain their momentum, and if their offensive were to fail, they would lose their foothold in the area.

Before I had left Damascus for Homs, Darren White – a security and military expert in London – had explained to me the precision of this kind of fighting. It looks simple – moving around buildings, taking small pieces of land. But according to White, 'it requires control, command and micromanagement. It's what the Russians did when they took the Reichstag building during the battle of Berlin in the spring of 1945. It took ten days to secure one building.'

By the autumn of 2012, the Syrian Army was winning in Homs. But they were a conventional army, they were trained in the conventional manner. They come from across the country: this was not their home. The FSA were locals, they knew the terrain, they could fight like guerrillas. They were defending the ground and had the advantage of defensive fire and coverage. Rifaf compared the rebels to boxers who jab at a fighter who is laid low. 'You annoy him, you take short, sharp, hit-and-run attacks. It's lethal.'

An hour goes by. A packet of cigarettes is nearly finished. You judge your time not by a wristwatch, but by how many cigarettes are lit. Every once in a while someone says something encouraging, like 'we'll get this school . . . eventually' or 'it's only a matter of time'.

The sun was sinking. Rifaf needed to talk to the commander, so we crept our way back to a street. Someone mentioned that Homs's finest high school was once here, pointing to a destroyed cluster of buildings. In another time, students sat in cafés drinking coffee or meandered through the streets with their backpacks. Now it looks like a post-apocalyptic *Mad Max* world of rocket-blasted buildings, skeletal structures – once homes – destroyed churches and front-line positions.

Shaza led the way into an old building the FSA rebels had just abandoned. It was located on another nearby front line. There were scattered medical supplies – empty bottles of painkillers, some used syringes, old bandages – and bloody clothing left behind. It used to be a triage hospital for wounded soldiers. Shaza disappeared and came back triumphantly from the corner of the room, showing me a rusted meat hook hanging from a doorframe.

'This is what the rebels used to torture *our* soldiers,' she says. 'They say we torture them – but they torture Assad soldiers they capture.' She pushed me forward into the room and made me examine the meat hook at close range. She pointed to the dried blood on it.

'You think we put it here?' she said, watching my face.

'I don't know. Did you?'

Shaza walked away.

This building, this former hospital that once treated FSA soldiers, fell after two days of fighting, an SAA soldier told me. The rebels abandoned the position in a matter of minutes when they realized they were defeated. They left behind two rusted IEDs – improvised explosive devices – some grimy, balled-up clothes, and one lone sneaker. There was a deep hole in the courtyard. Shaza stood next to it, peering inside, with one of the soldiers next to her.

'There's bodies down there,' she said, finally. 'That's where the FSA captured our Syrian boys, killed them and stuffed them down there.' She stood up and took my arm, urging me to move forward. She herself dropped back down on her knees, squinting into the darkened hole.

In East Timor, in Dili, during the violence in the aftermath of the 2000 referendum, some locals took me to a well in a lush, walled garden. They pushed me forward to see the bodies stuffed inside the well; they said there were dozens. I saw two or three, floating on top, purple and swollen and distended, but could see there were many more underneath, propping them up. A hand jutted through the water, and a foot. One of the locals had a long stick and was prodding the mass of dead flesh. They wanted me to take pictures, to write about it, they wanted to take me out onto the street to look at the other bodies that were floating up from the sewers and gutters.

I did so diligently, on autopilot, writing in my notebook, then climbing on my scooter that was driven by a former fisherman I had hired to work with me, and going to another part of town – finding more corpses. After a while, I stopped counting how many. They seemed to be everywhere – floating aimlessly in the sewers that I stepped over, in the road rotting, in the lush tropical bushes. It was so evil, that place, for such a place of voluptuous beauty. But the overwhelming memory for me of Timor was the bodies: and the smell of bodies rotting in the sun, like Rwanda.

Shaza said no one knew who had been in the hole before, or how many, or where they came from. 'There's no bodies there now,' she said, still on her knees peering down. She suggested we go and talk to the senior 'officer', who was in another building, one which we could climb through some more walls to reach.

General Baba was in his 'office', a burnt-out shop that had once sold furniture. He was in his forties, came from Tartus, on the coast, and was the son of an Alawite farmer. He had been on the front for weeks.

He wouldn't tell how many men were under his command. 'That's classified,' he said, like a recording. He asked one of his soldiers to make us coffee on a camp stove, and it was surprisingly good. He added three teaspoons of sugar to his cup and lit a cigarette.

'Have you been to Tartus?' he asked, genuinely interested. 'It's very beautiful. You shouldn't just see the warring parts of Syria.' He talked of his home town like a travel guide – as if there were no war.

I had once stayed with friends in Tartus, Sunnis who were loyal to Assad, in their beach-front apartment. It was the early days of the war, and they were in the first stages of denial that their countrymen were killing each other. They took me down to their apartment on the beach to get away from the tension in Damascus, and we drove through the green Alawite heartland, stopping at several different cafés, simple places with wooden tables and chairs that overlooked the mountains.

We arrived late at night, and the next morning we walked to the beach and waded slowly into the Mediterranean. Looking back, I could see the coast that stretches towards Gaza, towards Libya. We slept with the windows open, and it was quiet. But in the morning their elderly mother sat by a radio and said there was heavy fighting reported outside Damascus. The wife said the road would be closed. We packed quickly, cut the trip short, and drove back to the capital.

General Baba grew up not far from that beach. When I described it to him, he nodded happily: 'That's it – my family's house is not far from there.' He had Sunni friends, he says, and Shias and Jews and Christians. 'As children, we used to sing, all of us used to sing, "One, one, one, all Syrians are one".'

The other soldiers remembered the song, and one of them began to sing it.

'We did not think sectarian,' General Baba says. 'I know you don't believe me, but it's true.'

He drank another coffee and smoked another cigarette. There was a call on his radio, and his face darkened. Someone had been killed.

'I have to go,' he said. 'Another attack has started over there.' He pointed. 'And you should leave too, or you will be here for the next two days straight.'

How many men had he lost since this started?

Baba did not answer at first. Finally, he said: 'A huge number.'

After I left him, I ran through the back alleys and worked my way back to my car, back to the last safe street. It was about a fifteen-minute sprint from the front line. I parked the car in a little enclave called Almahatta, and it was pleasantly quiet, pleasantly peaceful. There were college students in neat headscarves and carefully pressed blue jeans drinking smoothies and smoking shisha. If there were peace, we would be able to sit with Rifaf and drink a coffee like normal people, in a café.

Less than twenty-four hours later, Rifaf and his unit took the school. Overnight, the FSA sent more snipers to defend their post, but Rifaf said they 'took them out'. He did not seem happy with the victory. Everyone was too exhausted.

'We finished the battle at 5 a.m.,' he said, his voice raspy. 'I've got to sleep because we have to start again later in the day. I've got a sore throat. I'm getting sick. I gotta go.' I didn't see Rifaf again, but I could still hear the sharp sound of the sniper's rifle, and still smell Rifaf's cigarette smoke in my hair.

Shaza wanted me to talk to some 'ordinary people'.

'I'm so happy there is traffic,' she said cheerfully. This means people are coming out of their houses, and no longer hiding from bullets. Homs is Syria's third-largest city, and it isn't an expansive place. Still, we sat in traffic for about an hour to get to the town hall. Shaza wanted me to see how people are working 'wartime shifts', meaning they come in for half a day and swap their positions with other workers who will pick up where they left off – there aren't enough desks or computers to go around.

She took me to have coffee with a friend of hers.

'Some people here hate,' said Mayada, an Ismaili (a minority group among Shias) married to an Alawite named Saadij. She was making us tea in her second-floor apartment in another neighbourhood of Homs. 'But some get much closer to each other because there are people like me who stay neutral. We bond with our neighbours because we are all fed up. You hear about Homs, the battlefield. But how about the people who just learn to live with the bombs?'

Saadij came into the room where we were sitting. 'This is the land of Moses, Mohammed and Jesus,' he said. 'We always taught our children to be Syrian first. Not Alawite. Just to be good boys. Good Syrians. Good people. People think we will kill each other, but we raised our kids to love, not hate.'

'But over there,' I said, pointing towards Bab al-Sebaa Street, 'they are fighting a war of hate.'

'They are fighting for politicians and proxy countries, not because they hate each other,' Saadij said.

'The FSA says they are fighting for freedom,' I added.

Saadij says, 'They can keep their freedom if this is the price we pay.'

By late October, the second year into the war, people started creeping back to Homs because they had no choice. Many had left and fled across the border – with smugglers or in trucks and buses to Lebanon. But 20 to 30 per cent of the pre-war population – about 10,000 people – came back to try to find their homes and rebuild their lives.

It was a maze of a city, a labyrinth, a tangle of destruction – then you passed a checkpoint, or an area that was completely destroyed, and found leafy streets with elegant houses that seem untouched, with courtyards and balconies and the jasmine plants still blooming. Near Baba Amr or Bab al-Sebaa the buildings were gutted and people were living on the front line. In the early morning light, I saw women tugging on their headscarves, gathering wood for fuel, or scouring the garbage for food. It was like Aleppo.

On a last trip to Bab al-Sebaa, I met a woman pushing a ten-month-old baby in a broken-down pushchair. One wheel was stuck, and the pushchair shuddered when she tried to push it. The expression on her face seemed frozen in torment. We stopped and talked. There was a time when she left, she said, when the bombing was too much to take. But her husband stayed in Homs, and she came back and put the children in a wartime school, and they got used to walking to it during bombings. Like the town hall workers, they would go in shifts, so that all the children got a chance to learn at least something. There was a shortage of teachers, books, paper, pens, of 'everything', she said.

As we were talking, her eleven-year-old son Abdullah greeted her. He was on his way home from his school shift.

'He's been here the entire time the war has gone on,' his mother said. 'I'm not sure he is the same boy.'

'I heard all the bombs, I just waited,' he said.

'What were you waiting for, *habibi*?' his mother asked, using the sweetest term of endearment – darling, sweetie.

He shrugged and picked a scab on his wrist.

'For it to end?'

He did not respond.

Near the front line, across the street from Bab al-Sebaa church, which was destroyed in the spring, is a little shuttered house. Everything around it is rubble; but Carla, who is thirty-two and a Christian, is living inside it with her children, in the home that she refuses to abandon. She invites us inside, opens the shutters, opens the doors. It is very cold, and her child coughs. The house is in near-darkness.

Carla fled briefly in November 2011, when the fighting was more brutal. She couldn't take it any more, and the children were hiding under the beds. Then she came back. 'Where were we supposed to go?'

Her husband, who worked in Homs's petroleum plant, stayed during the worst of the battle to protect the house, but Carla went to the countryside with her children. She hated it. She was frightened for her husband; she was frightened she wouldn't be able to find food for the kids; she was frightened for the future. She did not want to be alone. She came back to the centre of the war to keep the family united. They live off canned goods that they had from before the war, sacks of rice, some pasta – whatever they can find. 'You learn how to exist with war ways,' she says.

All of her children are traumatized in different ways, she explained. Some were wetting the mattress where they slept on the floor. Some of them would scream in their sleep. Her four-year-old, Nadem, began losing her hair.

'Let me tell you what helpless is: helpless is being a mother and not helping your kids.' Carla stared out of the window towards the church. It was peppered with bullet holes and there was a hole in the roof.

'Let's go inside,' she said, tonelessly. 'I want to show you. Let's go see what war does to everyone, even a church.' She actually believed that, because they lived opposite a church, they would somehow be spared the war. But the church had also been hit by bombs and bullets.

Inside, the pews were splintered and broken. Except for one icon of Mary, and a few scattered prayer books, everything had been burned and destroyed by shellfire. There was a small safe in the priest's side room, which had been pried open.

We wandered through the rubble. Nadem wanted to be picked up. Carla bent down and scooped the child into her arms.

'People were still praying here in March,' Carla said. 'They were coming to mass. Then, in a moment, the church was gone.'

A pitched battle had started on the next street, and Carla wanted to take the children inside. We walked back to her house, glass crunching under our feet. In the courtyard was a broken marble statue of Mary and Jesus.

At home, the children did not react to the machine-gun fire, which was coming in with greater frequency.

Naya, Carla's twelve-year-old, looked hunched and ancient. She said to no one in particular: 'Nobody knows where this war is going. But it has to go somewhere.'

'Doesn't it have to go somewhere, Mama?' Naya repeated. 'Doesn't it, Mama?'

Carla was silent.

'Mama?'

Then there was a renewed burst of machine-gun fire, and Naya went quiet.

8

Aleppo – Sunday 16 December 2012

Every afternoon, I saw him. He never changed: not his position, not his posture, not his clothes. Aleppo was desperate
in those months, and he, this old man on the road to the
hospital, buried up to his waist in trash, seemed to me the
symbol of all that was dying in that city. He was standing in a
field of garbage, his hands buried deep in some box, foraging.
He was scavenging for something to eat.

We were driving in a battered car we had picked up in
Turkey, with a driver called O., a nervous, small-boned Syrian
man, towards the small hospital that remained open in the
faintly lit darkness. Someone in the car, one of my colleagues,
either Paddy or Nicole, said, 'I've seen that guy before – he's
there every day.' The old man was always in the same place.
In the same position. Bent, broken.

Did he ever find anything?

I don't think so. But he kept coming back.

We had come together to Aleppo, the three of us – Nicole,
who was small and brave, from Hong Kong, who wrapped
her long hair in a dark scarf, and set off with her cameras
alone to front lines to look for her friend, Jim Foley; and

Paddy, who was English, and calm. We wanted to write about what people were eating, whether they were starving, how they survived.

The answer was, virtually nothing. On this winter day, there was no power to bake bread: there was no cooking gas. Life here was about deprivation, the driver told us, about yearning, wanting, forgoing. It was about memory and forgetting.

Once, a photographer friend of mine, trying to describe Afghanistan during the Mujahedeen years, called it The Land of the Elastic Hour. I understood instantly what he meant. There are places where time either races ahead like a finely tuned car, or remains impotent. Here in Aleppo, memory is elastic. Sometimes during wartime, minutes are endless. It seems you will never move forward to the next day – a day when there might be cooking gas and a lull in shelling.

This sense of timelessness, of lost time, is set against the fact that Aleppo is ancient – 7,000 years old, and imbued with history. The chronology of the oldest continuously inhabited city on earth stretches back to the latter half of the third millennium BC.

Archaeologists digging in the Mesopotamian ruins found tablets that spoke of the city's military power, its strength, its virility. Aleppo was the end of the Silk Road, weaving through Central Asia and Mesopotamia, a strategic trading point. The horses and caravans carried copper, wool, Chinese silk, spices from India, Italian glass, metal from Persia.

On this December day, three years into the war, I was looking for traces of Aleppo's former glory. I saw nothing but a weakened cavity, a shell. How could a city that was once the third-largest in the Ottoman Empire fade before one's eyes? On this day, a week before Christmas, when I should have been at home in Paris, putting up the Christmas tree with my small son, or shopping for presents and wrapping them in shiny paper, I was in a city that seemed apocalyptic.

The Battle of Aleppo seemed as if it would never end. The conflict was between Bashar al-Assad's government forces – combined with Hezbollah – and various Syrian opposition forces, largely composed of defected Syrian Army officers. I would like to list the components of the Syrian opposition, known as the rebels, but the recipe of warriors changes every day. There is internecine fighting. There is – as often happens in cities and communities that descend into war and anarchy – criminality as a means of survival.

At this point the opposition also included al-Nusra, or Jabhat al-Nusra (The Support Front for the People of Al-Sham), sometimes called Tanzim Qa'edat Al-Jihad fi Bilad Al-Sham, who are the al-Qaeda branch operating in Syria. They were formed in Syria in January 2012 and currently have an estimated 6,000 members.

The Islamic State, or ISIS – who would rise to power later in the war, to fight al-Nusra and the opposition and to drive parts of Syria and Iraq into 7th-century Islam with their brutal *sharia* law – were still somewhere in the shadows, embryonic. Nascent, waiting, forming.

Aleppo, the most industrial Syrian city, also once held the most diversified population. Before 2011, there were more

Christians here than in Beirut. There were Syrian Arabs, Kurds, Armenians, Assyrians, Turks, Circassians, Jews and Greeks. There are thirteen poetic references in the Bible to Aleppo (which from the eleventh century had the Hebrew name of Aram-Zobah).

From Psalm 60: 'to the chief Musician upon Shushan-eduth, Michtam of David, to teach; when he strove with Aram-naharaim, and with Aram-zobah, when Joab returned and smote of Edom, in the valley of Salt, twelve thousand.'

The Valley of Salt is about four hours from Aleppo on horseback, according to a slender document I have read, written by Henry Maundrell, a theologian who travelled the region in 1697. This is where David smote the Syrians.

Who is now smiting the Syrians? They are destroying each other. Brutally, horribly.

The regime forces, led by President Bashar al-Assad, use barrel bombs – a type of improvised explosive device (IED).[12] The bombs are like no other I have witnessed in the dozen or more wars I have lived through. They are unspeakably effective at causing pain: made from a barrel that is filled with shrapnel or chemicals, they are then dropped from a height by helicopter or aeroplane. Militants like them because they are cheap to make (sometimes costing under $300) and can easily be dropped on a highly populated civilian area, with severe consequences.

The image of the aftermath of a barrel bomb: knee-deep rubble, cries of agony, the frantic search for survivors; limbs dissected, muscles and pools of sticky blood. The fact of being alive in concrete, rubble, your legs broken, waiting for someone to dig you out. The entire weight of an apartment floor crushing your suddenly helpless and broken body.

I was waiting in front of the bakery in Handarat when I saw a helicopter roaming. It was 9.30 a.m. It circled in the air three times and then dropped the barrel bomb. It fell two metres from me. I saw it falling, but where could I hide? I felt the explosion. I felt the shrapnel going inside my leg . . . The shrapnel hit my neck and leg and my other leg was broken . . . I saw four injured people. They were moving on the ground. I was told in the field hospital that five or six people died.

Elias, seventeen years old, in a statement to Human Rights Watch[13]

Aleppo was a microcosm, in a sense, for the entire war in Syria: the Leningrad of the Syrian war. Or, as one rebel fighter told me, the 'Mother of All Battles'. It started here in much the same way as it did in Homs, in Hama, in Damascus, with pro-democracy rallies challenging Assad's autocratic rule, as part of the larger Arab Spring. It transformed from protests in 2011 to clashes in February 2012. At that point the rebels held the rolling countryside, bursting with crops in the summer, more barren in the winter, and it was still possible to drive from the Turkish border and pass through villages that had not yet been ravaged by war. Farmers were still at work, children still walked to school, tiny backpacks in place. Small schools, small houses: a normal life in a corner of what once was Mesopotamia.

In August 2012, in the heat and dust of northern Syria, the rebels had stormed Aleppo, and the intense fighting began. In this bleak month of December – four months later – opposition forces had cut off nearly all supply routes to Aleppo. Most of the UNESCO world heritage protected sites, such as the Old Town, were destroyed. The lives of the people living in Aleppo were destroyed, too.

There are two important criteria for staying alive here: hiding from the regime's barrel bombs, and finding food. On the government side, people have not been paid salaries and do not get humanitarian aid. On the rebel side, the portrait of daily life is equally bleak. No one respects ceasefires. As is so common in times of war, there is crime, distrust and sorrow.

No one seems to be able to end it, least of all the United Nations, whose peacemaking efforts have failed again and again. At the time of writing, in 2015, the third Special Envoy to Syria, Staffan de Mistura, an Italian-Swedish diplomat who had formerly worked in Afghanistan and Iraq, has been proposing that small local ceasefires, or 'freezings', will take place. But on the morning of 17 February 2015, when de Mistura was set to brief the United Nations Security Council in New York, the government forces launched a new offensive to cut off the main supply road to insurgents in Aleppo.

De Mistura had left Europe faintly confident – he had seen Assad in Damascus a few days before and had got his word that there would be a lull in the bombing for six weeks to allow humanitarian aid to pass through. De Mistura had also announced – to the horror of the Syrian opposition – that any political process would have to involve Assad. At dawn on 17 February, hours before de Mistura in New York got ready to lay out his freezing plan for Aleppo (which had, in part, been conceived by a young American analyst, Nir Rosen, who was working for an NGO called the Centre for Humanitarian Dialogue), the battle broke out.

Later, the rebels fought back. More dead, more bodies lying in the muddy winter of Aleppo. De Mistura gave a grim reading to a few UN reporters gathered outside the Security Council hall, but he would not take questions. Just like Kofi Annan and Lakhdar Brahimi, the two former special envoys, both veterans of ending prior wars, he looked defeated.

As reports were being read aloud in New York, and ambitious bureaucrats beavered away at their desks overlooking Lake Geneva, the history of Aleppo was fast disappearing. The souk and the covered bazaar, which date back to the fifteenth century and were carefully remodelled by governors and a Grand Vizier in the sixteenth century, served as a front line in this battle. In 2012, Stefan Knost,[14] a German historian who had taken part in excavations in pre-war Aleppo, said: 'We must unfortunately assume that either large sections of the bazaar have already been destroyed, or will be destroyed.' Three years later, there were snipers poised in crevices of the old walls, destruction, ruins.

The government forces stayed inside the Citadel, a fortified medieval palace once occupied by Greeks, Byzantines, Mamaluks. The government forces now use the walls of the former UNESCO world heritage site as barriers, and in the heights snipers nest, laying their rifles against the ancient stone.

What occurred inside those walls, in peaceful times when ancient people occupied it? But even history seems irrelevant now. The most important thing is to hide from bullets.

'The most difficult thing is not being able to feed your kids,' Umm Hamid said on my first night in Aleppo. She was a woman of average age, height, weight, everything indistinguishable under her full *abaya*. She had sallow skin, rough-pored and dirty hands, rubber slippers on her feet. We were in her home in Bustan al-Qasr, a neighbourhood between the old Citadel and the Queiq River, where civilians had been killed and tossed aside, their purple and swollen bodies floating on the tide.

Bustan al-Qasr was now a crossing-point between rebel-held and regime-held areas. There were snipers everywhere – positioned on the top floors of government buildings – and the streets were not safe. People needed to move between the two points, to work, to study – the University was on the regime-held side of the city – or to try to find food. There was a marketplace, but it too was targeted by snipers. To reach some buildings, you had to climb through holes that had been knocked out, or rather bombed out, of the walls, and you reached the other side from the inside. Rabbit warrens, little tunnels, short cuts to trick death.

As in Sarajevo during the siege, people used inoperative buses and piled sandbags to try to shield themselves from the snipers. It looked strange at first, then you got used to seeing them and they appeared normal. When we left our car to get to Umm Hamid's flat, we moved quietly, heads down, silently and quickly. It was always a relief to get into the car, even though in reality a sniper's bullet or a rocket or anything else can cut through the side door or window.

In a few months' time, O., our driver, would be badly injured in exactly that manner, in this same car, in this same city. It would take him a year to recover from his bullet wounds, his broken bones.

By the time I arrived in Aleppo, every neighbourhood was now a fiefdom, dictated by political survival and black-market criminality. The people were caught in the middle. It wasn't clear who was in control of Bustan al-Qasr that week. In August, it was Ahrar Surya, one of the city's largest rebel brigades. No one knew who was in charge on the day I arrived.

O. whispered: 'Best not to ask too many questions.' He found his gun under the car seat, and slid it back under, further away from the foot well. I asked him not to carry it – he stared back at me wordlessly as if to say, you know nothing.

Through the dirty car windows splattered with rain and mud, I could see Umm Hamid's flat from the street, her main window that faced out lit up by candles inside. Nicole went first, then Paddy, then me, up four flights of stairs to the apartment in the dark, the wet tiled floors slippery and cold. Her children stood at the end of one room, shivering. I saw a row of tiny, dirty, tear-streaked faces.

We stretched out sleeping bags in the front room. Through her windows, the street looked baneful: empty except for a few people carrying torches, illuminating small puddles near their feet with a pale yellow light. There were thuds of shelling and the occasional pop of a sniper's gun. A few FSA – Free Syrian Army – rebel fighters gathered on the corner.

Umm Hamid is a 'laqab' (an Arabic epithet that identifies a person), meaning Mother of Hamid. Her husband was a local sheikh, regarded with respect in the neighbourhood as a decision-maker, someone to trust. Their address had been given to us via safe contacts as a place we could trust, arranged through SMS from the Turkish border via local mobile phones. *How safe is your apartment? When will your husband be back? Will we be able to stay with you without anyone knowing we are there? We'll arrive after dark so no one sees us.*

She made us tea and spoke of the children. 'When they wake up at night and want a glass of water, you can't give it to them,' she said, squatting on the floor and pouring the tea into dirty glasses. 'When they wake up at night and want to go to the bathroom, they can't. When they wake up at night and ask me to stop the bombs, I can't do that either.'

Then there was the lack of food. She spoke of what she missed, of what she had lost, of what she felt she would never regain. 'Before the war, there were fruit trees,' she said, almost longingly. Then she began to talk about them, memory as a way of never forgetting. Apples, tangerines, pears and plums, pomegranates and jasmine.

Nights in Bustan al-Qasr were clamorous. There were more than a dozen people in the flat and the mixture of human sounds, coughing, crying, snoring, laughing, mingled with the shooting and detonations outside the window. When I woke up in the morning, wrapped in a sleeping bag in all my clothes, one of her smaller children was sobbing. She didn't want to go outside, she said in a broken voice. She was frightened. Please, Mama, she begged.

Umm Hamid dressed the crying girl. She stuffed her miniature hands into socks instead of gloves to keep them warm. She was taking her to queue outside the bakery in the Kadi Askar neighbourhood. There was no one to leave the girl with, she said unapologetically, so she was bringing her to stand in the line with her. They might be waiting all day, she told us.

'If we get there early, we might be lucky,' she whispered to the little girl.

If she were lucky, she would not be living in Aleppo. If she were lucky, she would not have to cook on a wood stove. If she were lucky, her children could play outside, or not be afraid of the balcony, where people shot at you when you stuck your head out. If she were lucky, her husband would not have been jobless for the past four months. If she were lucky, there would be no war.

The Arabic name for Aleppo is Halab. Some people say it means iron, or possibly copper, because the city was a source of these metals in ancient times. But there is also a biblical legend that Halab means 'the giver of milk', because Abraham allegedly gave out milk to travellers when they passed through the city.

But the city called the giver of milk has now ground to a halt, except for the fighting. Umm Hamid has not had milk at home for months. She had powdered milk, she said.

Eventually, Umm Hamid coaxed the protesting girl, holding her by the arm, and we followed her down the stairs. On the staircase, she saw her younger son wearing rubber sandals outside on the street instead of shoes. December is cold in Aleppo, covered by grey mud and raked by icy wind. She stared at him, but she did not go inside to get him socks: she did not have any. Nor did he have shoes.

She just stared at the boy's feet, purple with cold, then hurried on to the bakery. There was nothing for him to do, and nothing for her to say.

We took the small child to the market and bought him shoes, which he silently laced up. But he was one child. There were dozens, hundreds, thousands in Aleppo that did not have his tiny shred of luck that day.

War means endless waiting, endless boredom. There is no electricity, so no television. You can't read. You can't see friends. You grow depressed but there is no treatment for it and it makes no sense to complain – everyone is as badly off as you. It's hard to fall in love, or rather, hard to stay in love. If you are a teenager, you seem halted in time.

If you are critically ill – with cancer, for instance – there is no chemotherapy for you. If you can't leave the country for treatment, you stay and die slowly, and in tremendous pain. Victorian diseases return – polio, typhoid and cholera. You see very sick people around you who seemed in perfectly good health when you last saw them during peacetime. You hear coughing all the time. Everyone hacks – from the dust of destroyed buildings, from disease, from cold.

As for your old world, it disappears, like the smoke from a cigarette you can no longer afford to buy. Where are your closest friends? Some have left, others are dead. The few who remain have nothing new to talk about. You can't get to their houses, because the road is blocked by checkpoints. Or snipers take a shot when you leave your door, so you scurry back inside, like a crab retreating inside its shell. Or you might go out on the wrong day and a barrel bomb, dropped by a government helicopter, lands near you.

Wartime looks like this.

The steely greyness of the city. The clouds are so low, but not low enough to hide government helicopters carrying barrel bombs, which usually appear at the same time each day, in the mornings and late afternoons, circling for a while at altitudes of 13,000–16,000 feet, little more than tiny dots in the sky, before dropping their payloads.

What does war sound like? The whistling sound of the bombs falling can only be heard seconds before impact – enough time to know that you are about to die, but not enough time to flee.

What does the war in Aleppo smell of? It smells of carbine, of wood smoke, of unwashed bodies, of rubbish rotting, of the heady smell of fear. The rubble on the street – the broken glass, the splintered wood that was once somebody's home. On every corner there is a destroyed building that may or may not have bodies still buried underneath. Your old school is gone; so are the mosque, your grandmother's house, and your office. Your memories are smashed.

Then there are the endless fields of garbage. The rooms that are as cold as tombs – having gone unheated now for five winters – are all you know. There are so many abandoned apartments. Remember that beautiful house, what it looked like when someone lived there? Your beautiful life from before is now dead.

The dirt, filth, fear and nausea. All the things you go without – toothpaste, money, vitamins, birth-control pills, X-rays, chemotherapy, insulin, painkillers. Petrol costs 170 Syrian pounds per litre. Today. Tomorrow it might be different.

Then, suddenly, you might catch the odd sight of a man in a T-shirt despite the frozen air, squeezing oranges into juice for the lucky ones with money. Oranges? You wonder who the people are that still have money, and you have dark thoughts about people you used to trust and know well. But with the constant theme of survival surrounding your whole city, your neighbourhood, your life, you really don't know anybody's intentions.

War is the corner near the Old City where people are lined up with plastic Pepsi bottles, to buy a small amount of petrol on the black market. War is the wrecked hospital, Dar al-Shifa, bombed on 21 November 2012, which still stinks of carnage in hallways where stretchers once passed, and where doctors in scrubs and rubber gloves once walked. Now it is a twisted pile of cinderblocks and concrete, broken tiles and glass – a shell exposed to the grey sky.

War is empty shell casings on the street, smoke from bombs rising up in mushroom clouds, and learning to determine which thud means what kind of bomb. Sometimes you get it right, sometimes you don't.

War is the destruction, the skeleton and the bare bones of someone else's life.

★   ★   ★

In 2006, Aleppo won the title of Islamic City of Culture awarded by the Islamic Educational Scientific and Cultural Organization (ISESCO). Historic landmarks were restored. Tourism was up. Aleppo was going to be the new Marrakesh, an exotic destination with pleasant weather, boutique hotels, interesting restaurants and direct flights from Paris or London. An exotic, Eastern city with beguiling buildings made from gold-coloured stone.

Aleppo was famous for its olive-oil soap and its refined houses in the old city. Encouraged by the well-dressed willowy wife of Bashar al-Assad, Asma – who had been profiled in a glowing article in American *Vogue* just before the government ordered security forces to fire on unarmed protesters – fashion designers, artists and writers who were her friends began to buy property. In Paris, just before the Arab Spring, I met the most elegant people who were proud to be flying to Aleppo to buy art and furniture. When the protests started, and I phoned them to ask about what had happened to Aleppo, to their homes, to their parties, they would not take my calls.

But I have seen this happen before. The celerity with which life as you know it breaks down is overwhelming. The beautiful people stop coming. The water stops, taps run dry, banks go, and a sniper kills your brother. There is nowhere to seek recourse, and barely time to grieve before you see a helicopter flying in the sky and hear the thwack of another bomb. You get used to hallucinations appearing in broad daylight. The dead and mangled return to you, over and over, and not just in dreams. Once you see one dead body – the shoes ripped off from the force of an explosion – you never forget what it looks like.

But what you don't expect is that ordinary things – those things that you take for granted in life – disappear too. The man who collects the rubbish no longer comes because there are no functioning civil services. The nurses who draw blood disappear because the hospitals are bombed. Your daily newspaper, your coffee shop, then – eventually – every bit of normality you know is gone.

What you yearn for more than anything is for the ordinary to return. The simple pleasure of going to a shop to buy apples; to smoke a cigarette languidly in a café; the ease of a university student driving from one side of the city to the other to get to her psychology or macroeconomics class without encountering a round of gunshots.

When I think back on my time in Aleppo, the strongest memory I have is of watching the baby die. I have my own child at home. He is healthy and lives in the first world; he drinks milk and eats cookies before bed, studies by an electric light, goes skiing, plays with Lego. He does not know war. His heroes are the heroes of *Star Wars* – the good and evil, the Jedi and the Senators, Darth Vader, Luke Skywalker and Princess Leia. His heroes are not jihadists, fighters, or people who get through the front lines bearing humanitarian aid.

The suffering of children is particularly painful for anyone, but for me, as a mother, when I look into the eyes of the mothers whose children are helplessly dying, I feel like a fraud. I watch this, then I can go home.

It did not take long for this infant in Aleppo to die, maybe ten minutes, possibly even less. The doctor, Khaled – who is so young, only a resident – and the nurses worked on him.

They tried desperately to keep the tiny bundle alive. He had come in with a simple respiratory infection. Nothing drastic, not a gunshot wound, not an artery severed by shrapnel.

I watched them huddled over his body. It was like watching an Olympic race: Khaled's face tense and full of competitive anticipation, the nurses next to him in their hijabs and sneakers. They were competing against time, against death.

But they were losing. They checked the dying baby's fading eyes with a battered flashlight; they took his pulse, and gently thumped the bottoms of his feet to test his reflexes.

But he was gone. Nicole and Paddy and I watched, standing on the side, feeling awkward and in the way, as the life went out of this baby: someone that had been on this earth the moment before was suddenly, irrevocably, dead. Nicole did not touch her cameras; Paddy stood on one side.

Then it was over. His breathing just stopped. The thread was cut.

Now that we were back in the emergency room, I could hear the screams of other people in pain. I was aware of the coldness of my feet against the marble floor and someone else's blood on the wall. Against my will, I began to cry, with a kind of rush of tears dripping off my face onto my down coat. I could not stop them, with tissues or with Nicole's startled glance at me, imploring me to get a grip. I summoned the urge to be in control, but it was impossible. I went into a small room, practically a cupboard, where they kept supplies. Nicole joined me after a moment.

'You OK?'

A nod. She handed me a fresh tissue. I was thinking of my boy, how he had been born seven weeks premature and how, if he had been born in Aleppo, and not Paris, he would probably be dead.

At the time of that child's death, there were only thirty-one doctors for one million people in Aleppo. Khaled had been promoted by management somewhere – whatever was left of management – from being a resident to heading the hospital. He asked me not to write the name of it, or its location in Aleppo, 'because then it will be bombed', like Dar al-Shifa, a hospital that had been deliberately targeted a few weeks before by government bombs because it was heavily used by civilians.

Targeting public spaces during wartime, especially those that are known to be full of civilians – hospitals, schools, etc. – is a violation of the Geneva Convention. But who here cares about the Geneva Convention? Are Assad's bombers who fly the planes low enough in the sky to drop the bombs, even aware of the Geneva Convention? Has any war ever taken into account the Geneva Convention?

Khaled had a terrible look of defeat on his face as he wrapped the small, dead baby in a triangular blanket, covering the lifeless head before turning to the mother.

She was also young, sitting quietly in a chair next to the examining table, wearing a hijab and a thick brown *abaya*. Her skin was faintly yellow. Hepatitis? Jaundice? Or just malnourishment, lack of sleep, lack of water and fresh air and good food?

The mother shivered slightly in the cold of the darkened emergency room, but she seemed to be in the kind of pain that goes beyond tears. She looked hollow.

She took the wrapped package, her baby. Her husband touched her shoulder. They stood, with a kind of stooped dignity, and left the room.

'The thing is,' Khaled said, turning to me, his glasses on slightly crooked, 'that the baby died of a respiratory infection.' A respiratory infection that might have responded to a massive antibiotic drip in another country. Nothing serious, nothing that could not be handled. Outside of wartime.

The parents had waited until the baby had barely any life in him before they brought him in: there had been too much shelling in the city and they feared being killed by a rocket as they made their way from their home to the hospital.

What Khaled needed, he said, are ambulances. They cost $40,000 each and would get the wounded and the critically ill to the hospital faster. 'It's not really asking for a lot, is it?' he asked. 'One ambulance?'

We kept going back to the hospital at different hours of the day. The same nurses and Khaled were working. More patients. Another woman was brought into the ER suffering from spasms. Her body was convulsed, her legs and arms shook with tremors as a friend tried to quiet her. Her relatives said she had had cerebral palsy from birth, but her condition was worsening – her lungs were filling with fluid, she could not breathe. They each took one of her hands and tried to calm her, steady her.

Then she saw us, Westerners, trying to make ourselves small in a corner, and she screamed out, 'If I die, take my children!' She clutched her stomach as though she was having an appendicitis attack. She gave a high-pitched shrill shriek: 'Take them with you! Take them with you!'

Another relative dragged her away.

Khaled had been known in his high school days as a champion foosball (table football) player. After calming the woman, he took off his glasses, rubbed his eyes and said he was taking a break. He had been working since dawn – he was on a twenty-four-hour shift.

He climbed up the four flights to the small abandoned part of the hospital near the roof – no one wants to be near the roof because of bombing, but the doctors took over this space to sleep and eat in between shifts. He told us to follow. There was a foosball table – old, but still workable – on the top floor. Foosball, beloved by European kids. Khaled stood over it, fiddling with the knobs. Something resembling a smile seemed to cross his face.

One of the nurses had made a pot of soup from beans, and someone else had brought bread. The hospital had two things going for it: they got petrol from the FSA to keep the generators going long enough to do surgery, using headlamps to light up their patients' bodies, and they got bread.

'Grateful for small miracles,' Khaled said, dipping a spoon into the bowl. It did not taste so bad: it was thick and, most importantly, it was hot.

He didn't want to talk about the baby, or about the city or the war. 'I'd like to think about something outside of here,' he said. All he would say about the baby was that if it had been peacetime, he would have lived.

There was a tiny girl with us in the room, a local celebrity of sorts. She was a singer. At demonstrations, her brothers and sisters marched her in front of the crowd and she sang protest songs in a stunningly clear voice. She ate a bowl of soup that someone handed her, and then began to sing. Everyone clapped to the rhythm of her song. She closed her eyes and held up her hands and moved in a kind of trance.

Khaled was singing, too, but he looked wasted. 'I can't cope,' he said after a while, and went to bed in one of the hospital cots downstairs. 'See you in the morning.'

A year after I met Khaled, he was married, and his young wife had just given birth in Turkey. I called to ask him about a polio epidemic that had apparently broken out in Syria. He said that his newborn baby had given him hope. 'There is not much hope left in Syria,' he said.

'Are you going back?'

'How can I stay away?' he responded.

Salat is the obligatory Muslim prayers, performed five times each day by the devout. The first, called *Salat al-Fajr,* is at dawn. Prayer takes place again at midday after the sun passes higher. This is called *Salat al-Zuhr. Salat al-Asr* comes in the late part of the afternoon, *Salat al-Maghrib* soon after sunset, and finally the *Salat al-Isha* between sunset and midnight.

The other pillars of Islam are *shahada,* faith; *zakat,* giving savings to the poor; *sawm*, fasting; and *hajj*, the pilgrimage to Mecca. But none affects daily life more than the *salat* in both war and peace.

I have seen soldiers in trenches stop to pray, and farmers in fields, and even my translators have asked to be excused in mid-sentence when they are called to pray.

We had moved apartments, from Umm Hamid's to a secure house in another neighbourhood, where some FSA rebel soldiers and activists were living. The men here prayed reverently. They gathered together in the main room to pray, eat, talk, and, in between, to strategize on their computers.

They were quiet when Nicole and I walked by to use the bathroom – a good one, we said, it was a hole in the ground, but it was ceramic and it was clean – or to make tea on a stovetop, when there was cooking fuel. We had to stay in our room to eat dinner. A neighbour woman left the food on the floor outside our door on a tray, and we picked it up and sat on our beds to eat. I knew we were not prisoners, but I sensed what it might feel like to be a woman in their world.

Today there was a funeral. It was near midday – the sun had not come out at all – when the call of the muezzin broke the cold greyness of the sky. At the graveyard, called Martyrs Field, in the neighbourhood of Salah al-Din, a man named Mohammed stopped to pray. He worked in the grave-yard every day. Sometimes, he took his small redheaded son with him to the cemetery. He wore high rubber boots as he scooped up earth with his shovels, laying down the bodies in their bloody blankets, and then covering them with more earth.

I was worried for the redheaded child, surrounded by the dead, the haunting he will find later in his life when he combs through the memories – if he lives. If he gets through today, this week, this month, this year.

Sheikh Moisin, a religious leader working with Mohammed, says that the bodies sometimes have no heads. Sometimes, he says, they have no faces.

'And your boy sees this?' I say quietly to Mohammed. He looks confused.

'It doesn't bother him,' he answers. 'Death is like life.'

But not in wartime.

Part of the graveyard used to be a park. But the death toll in Aleppo demanded more room for burials. As of January 2015, the United Nations estimated the figure of the total number of deaths in Syria since the outbreak of the conflict at 220,000; but others give higher figures.

Here in Aleppo, the playground-turned-cemetery was essential. Sentiment was put aside and the ground was readied to accept bodies, rather than to have children play. It is so unlike Montparnasse Cemetery in Paris, near where I live, which I often walk through, or, in the spring, ride my bicycle through, in order to think. It is not like the cemetery in America where my father, sister and two brothers are buried, where my mother goes at Christmas, Easter, and on their birthdays to lay flowers and wreaths. It is where the dead go during wartime.

'It is my duty, my work of God, to bury the dead,' Mohammed said simply. He is a man completely devoid of drama. He says he does not have nightmares from his work, nor is he afraid of the dead.

The redheaded child, who turned out to be only four years old, clung to his father's hand – when there wasn't a shovel in it. Wouldn't the little boy remember mutilated corpses, children's crushed and twisted bodies, or those dead faces caught in the agony of the last moments of their lives?

'Death is death,' Sheikh Moisin said. 'The dead cannot hurt you.'

On the day I visited Mohammed, he was burying a man who, an hour before, had been alive. Muslims try to bury their dead before sunset on the same day, so as to honour the dead: the bathing, the enshrouding in white; the funeral prayer; the positioning of the head towards Mecca. But this is war. Two hours ago, this man had been on the front line, fighting. Then a bomb blew him up. His life was extinguished, fast, like a candle.

He had not been bathed, but someone brought a bloody blanket to wrap him in. Friends brought him to the cemetery, but only three people were standing at the edge of the shallow grave dug by Mohammed.

His corpse was wrapped but his head was exposed. He had fair hair, a pleasant look about him, and slightly bucked teeth. His eyes were ringed with purple bruises – a result of the explosion? The gravedigger shrugged, and asked one of the three men to say their prayers.

'He's smiling,' one of the men finally said, after he had prayed. 'The martyr is smiling.'

A martyr, killed in *jihad*, holy war. A *shaheed*.

'He's not smiling,' another man interjected. 'He looks shocked. The bomb got him when he was not looking.'

'No, you're wrong. The martyr is smiling.'

'If he's smiling, it means he is going to heaven,' the third man said.

The gravedigger said quietly: 'What we know is he is leaving Aleppo.' He pushed the last bit of earth on the grave, shutting out the sky.

From Salah al-Din, we drank some tea to get warm and then drove to the broken-down Old City. A man was selling the usual plastic Pepsi bottle of petrol. A tiny girl walked by him, wearing pyjamas, holding the hand of her even tinier brother. She could be no older than five. Where was she going? She said she had been sent out to look for food.

In the yellow winter light the scavengers were back in the rubbish dump near our new apartment, picking through the mountain of trash for anything that might help them survive. Children were chopping down trees in the park for firewood. The tree stumps looked darkly deformed, grotesque. The kids wore the rubber slippers usually worn by the poolside in tropical climates, and no socks. They slipped as they walked on the freezing ice, the hardened mud.

Later in the day, before dark, we went to the bread queue at Kadi Askar. The people standing there were the same as those that had been there that morning. Now they were colder, hungrier and angrier. The bakery itself was surrounded by barbed wire. It was to keep people out, since starving people will do anything. People's faces change to desperation when they wait for food. Some waited with a book, others just looked empty, hollow, aching.

It was raining. Cold, fat, freezing drops of rain were falling, but very few people had umbrellas.

The next day, 17 December 2012, the temperature dropped below zero. I remembered my life during the war in Sarajevo, and I wondered if someone here in Aleppo, as in Sarajevo, was recording everything that was happening in the city: who lived, who died, the temperature, how many shells fell, who took what ground. I wondered if someone was keeping a Book of the Dead. That day in Aleppo, without newspapers, radio, TV or Internet, I knew from talking to people that the Free Syrian Army still held around 60 to 70 per cent of the city and were battling to take an old fort outside of town. I knew from watching them that every time there was an explosion, the people in the bread queue shifted slightly. It is terrifying when people no longer react to gunfire, so accustomed are they to its sound.

I knew that people were sickened and weary of war, but what I did not know was that two years later, if I had been able to project into the future, the same thing would be happening. The war would not be over.

All of the stories would be similar. 'I walked into a room and I saw a government soldier with a gun,' said Ahmed, a wounded FSA soldier, waiting near me.

'I couldn't kill him so he tried to kill me.' He paused and stared down at the missing half of his leg. Ahmed was unable to shoot at a young boy near his own age, who in a different world might have sat next to him in a classroom. Seeing

Ahmed's hesitation, the boy had shot at him, blowing off half of his leg.

'Isn't that a nice story?' Ahmed said, his face rigid with pain, before turning away.

In the bread queue the people talked only of the war.

'I have been here five hours.'

'I have been here six.'

They looked for faces they recognized; the faces they knew from before, of neighbours, aunts, uncles and cousins. No one was recognizable any more. I thought of the Stalin years, how the poet Anna Akhmatova wrote of the queues, of the waiting, of the pain of seeing the people she loved standing in line and being unable to recognize them because of the sorrow that had indelibly been etched into their features.

This was the only 'opposition bakery' – meaning a bakery that was not held by the Syrian government and that was run in an opposition neighbourhood. People going there were hungry, rather than political, but they were still angry with the leaders – and not just with Assad. They were angry with the opposition leaders, with the lack of political leadership, with the West, with China and Russia who support Assad, and with the 'guys with the beards' – the radical jihadists who would soon turn out to be a part of the Islamic State.

They were even angry with us reporters sitting in our beaten-up car. Nicole had been born in Hong Kong, and even though her hair was wrapped in a hijab, when they saw her face, they grew angry. China, along with Russia, had blocked the UN Security Council action against Syria. They began to scream and pound at the car window.

What has Nicole got to do with the UN Security Council? Nothing.

But a crowd's anger is terrifying, and O., the driver, reached for his gun, which was more frightening, because if he had a gun, certainly those in the crowd did too. I told him to put it away, and Paddy quietly talked him down. We finally climbed out of the car in a little tunnel made of people trying to help us, and ran into the bread factory.

Another man named Mohammed, who had been a car mechanic before the war, managed the bakery. Mohammed had a thankless task. If the bread didn't rise, if the petrol didn't arrive to start the generator, if there was not enough bread to be sold, the crowd turned on him. The Assad government had sent messages that he would be kidnapped, tortured and killed if he kept running the bakery. He had not listened, he said. He was too busy baking bread.

He shrugged. 'The bread needs to rise so I keep working,' he said. 'And it takes five hours to rise.' He wiped flour off his trousers and led us towards the enormous mixing bowls. He was not afraid of Assad's thugs, or the criminals who threatened him, or even the FSA bullies. He showed up at daybreak every day at the bakery – a cavernous hole of a former factory – to start the process: getting the generators going, turning on the machines, mixing the flour and water, supervising the barren, empty place.

There were only about five people working there – he couldn't afford to pay any more, and no one could make it across the nearby front lines to get in to work. The equipment was ancient.

'If you have a crisis, a war like this,' he said, 'you need to work. Otherwise you think about nothing but the war all day long. I would rather think about bread.' Together, Mohammed and his little team made about 17,000 bags of bread a day – each bag containing fourteen loaves of flat bread. He said this bread was keeping Aleppo alive.

Before threatening to kill him, 'the regime offered me money not to make the bread, so that the people would starve', he said. But now he was protected by the FSA. 'I'd be dead if they didn't,' he said. They even gave him flour and salt, and petrol to run the generator.

Our lives, he told me, depend on whether we can get petrol for the generators.

Imagine this, he said in an exhausted voice. 'Every step I take, everything I do is about whether or not I can get petrol for the generator. I have to feed a city on that hope. Every single day.'

At dusk, pink shapes came out of the shadows. It was now twilight, the hour of the wolf, the hour between the wolf and the dog. Faint stars appeared.

Earlier in the day, in the early morning light, we had dragged our flak jackets, helmets and backpacks stuffed with supplies for a day or longer (water, power bars, an emergency blanket using plastic sheeting sprayed with aluminium, a medical kit) into the back of O.'s beaten-up car. We headed towards Zarzour Hospital.

The chief doctor seemed friendly at first. He invited me to a room to talk, but then, when we sat on the cracked and cold leather chairs, he looked at me with the hardened eyes of an abandoned animal. He had been working all day and, before that, all night. His body language was of utter defeat, exhaustion. Not just the clear half-moons of darkness under his eyes, but the way his arms hung from his body – weightless. The fatigue of his work bored into his physical being.

'Hundreds of people in here in the past month because of missile attacks,' he said, his voice rising in anger. 'Where is the United Nations? When is the international community coming to save us?' He said the UN had promised that hospitals would not be bombed.

But I am not the UN, I protested, and he cut me off.

'But they are bombing! They are still bombing hospitals!'

I opened my mouth to say something, but any excuse I had was feeble. I shut it and remained silent. The doctor shifted forward in his seat, inched his body closer, and pointed his finger at me.

'Where are they?' he demanded. 'Where is the UN? Who is coming to save us?'

'The UN is not coming,' I said finally. 'You must not wait for anyone. You have to save yourself.'

He stared at me for the longest time. Then he jumped to his feet. He went to the door and asked me to leave. I gathered my things, embarrassed, and stood. As I walked down the hall, he shouted after me: 'One UN official, and only one, came and promised to help. He did nothing!'

All the way down the hall, he continued to shout. 'No one will ever do anything! They promise everything, they do nothing!! We have had enough. We will be alone, as we always have been.'

But I know, I wanted to tell him. I know that we have done nothing. And this is the worse part of it – when you realize that what separates you, someone who can leave, from someone who is trapped in Aleppo, or Homs or Douma or Darayya, is that you can walk away and go back to your home with electricity and sliced bread; then you begin to feel ashamed to be human.

That night, in the darkened apartment lit by torches, I met a young American journalist. He had curly hair and glasses, and was rotund in a childlike way. He was also funny and seemed more light-hearted than the rest of us; a relief from the day at the bakery. His name was Steven Sotloff. He was travelling with a researcher from Washington named Barak; they both spoke Arabic and were working together.

Steve had lived in Yemen, where he had studied Arabic and lived in the Old City. It had been lonely; he had been broke, and he talked about eating potato sandwiches. He and Barak sparred and spoke in jokes. They reminded me of Laurel and Hardy.

Steve moved from Yemen to Benghazi. 'You lived in Benghazi full time?' I asked. 'So where do you go to the movies? How do you go out on a date?'

He laughed and laughed, and said his life was fucked up, like that of all foreign correspondents. 'Don't you wish you hadn't gotten obsessed with Syria?' he asked.

In another chair sat a photographer named Jason who had put together an achingly beautiful book about Russia. He was wearing all his clothes – his thick jacket, hat and thermal gloves – and sat quietly in the chair. He said he had travelled by bus from his home in Istanbul to Gaziantep. He sat with his cameras in his lap, watching, not talking.

Steve Sotloff, however, talked a lot. He told me was hungry, so I gave him a bag of my freeze-dried food – unappetizing silver packets of flavoured yogurt and muesli, and chicken in a bright yellow sauce I had bought in a camping shop near Saint-Germain in Paris. He ate it hungrily. He said he liked the taste.

His slangy language, his Americanism, in Aleppo, made me smile: the juxtaposition of words and place, his expressions, his kid-like curiosity. I forgot the cold, the anxiety, the gnawing fear in my stomach.

Steve and Jason were travelling cheap and needed rides, so they jumped on the backs of other drivers. Our fixer was a beautiful and nervous man called A. Neither Steve, nor I, trusted him entirely. Everything about A. was ambiguous and uncertain: his name, his age, his past experience as a soldier (it was unclear whether or not he was still fighting with the rebels and, if so, with which brigade). A French photographer had given me A.'s name, and I had contacted him, and arranged a meeting. A. promised, as best one could promise, to keep us safe. I did not entirely believe him.

Nicole wasn't sure either. She was only twenty-six, but had good instincts, having spent so much time in Syria, in Aleppo specifically. There was an old-soul quality about Nicole, youthful as she was. She was a sombre woman, quiet, restrained. She said she was in Aleppo to document the war, to photograph, but she was really here to search for her friend Jim Foley, a young journalist who had been kidnapped.

She had snippets of information – she had been waiting for Jim on the Turkish side of the border when he had disappeared nine weeks before – and she was trying to weave them together like a detective, tracing his last days, his last hours, trying to find out any more information that might bring him home. She talked about him, and as she did so, there was such tenderness in her friendship and her search for him. She loved him like a brother.

There was another young woman there, too, a Syrian girl, beautiful and voluptuous, with long flowing hair and eyes lined with kohl. She was what the French would call *pulpeuse*, and she spoke and moved with a kind of innate sensuality. She took my matted hair between her mittened hands and tried to comb it; she loaned me a lipstick, eyeliner, a hairbrush.

A. had lost his best friend a few days before we arrived on the front line. He broke down in tears at various intervals – when going out on the back terrace to start the wheezing generator, when talking to us about the situation in Aleppo. He smoked incessantly, never seemed to eat, poured out endless cups of tea. He dropped sugar cubes inside them, stirred, gulped, and poured another cup.

One night, the night of his friend's funeral, he and the Syrian girl sat up all night in the sitting room where Jason used to sleep in a chair. I heard them both intermittently laughing and crying, all night long.

When you saw them together, you could see how damaged they both were. Earlier when we were eating 'dinner' – the foil packets of freeze-dried food – A. said his heart was broken. He cried again, this time with great heaving sobs.

'It's too much,' he said, in English. He repeated it, louder: 'Too much.' The generator went out – again – and the room went dark. A. put on rubber slippers and went out on the patio in the rain to try to start it again. He couldn't get it going and he came back defeated.

'I'll get more petrol in the morning,' he said, then sat in a chair and said nothing.

That night, the two of them stayed up late. There was half a roast chicken on the table that A. had gone out to the dark street to buy from a vendor. It lay, greasy, on a piece of wax paper on the dusty table.

The two Syrians pushed their sleeping bags together on the floor and lay on their sides facing each other, whispering. Perhaps it was flirtation, though the girl said she had a boyfriend fighting somewhere on the front line, a powerful rebel commander, and that she was a woman of the revolution. Later, as I was trying to fall asleep, I could hear them smoking – crumpling the pack of cigarettes, striking a match, inhaling deeply, exhaling, and laughing. It was 2 a.m. The shooting outside was still going on, and a mortar landed somewhere. I finally fell asleep much later to the sound of the girl comforting A., who was sobbing once again. He sounded like a child, not a hardened fighter.

A few weeks later A. would be murdered while sitting in his car. That handgun he kept below the seat had not helped him. It was a crime related to factions within the rebel groups; it might have been a revenge attack, it might have been a robbery. No one seemed to know, and worse, no one was surprised.

O., the driver who had taken us back and forth to Aleppo neighbourhoods, to bread queues, to the Old City, had also been shot and badly wounded while driving his car. He survived.

I wrote to the beautiful Syrian girl, but she did not respond. Many months later, I had an email from her, a strange and disjointed message, asking me to join her somewhere inside Homs. In the email, she gave me a time and place, and said she would be waiting. It seemed like a trap, and I did not reply – I was suspicious, paranoid as everyone always is with messages that come out of Syria. I never saw her again, but many months later I got a message from her that she had not sent the message. Someone said it was a way that Nusra, and later ISIS, lured foreigners to be kidnapped.

Steve was the one to write to me about A.'s murder.

'I'm not shocked,' he wrote. 'I always felt a bit uncomfortable walking into his office. He had to have been a target. The people in the city are sick of the mess, and their feelings towards those helping journalists as much as he did must have been negative. I have lost so many friends in this war as well. It's hard to keep it from getting to you.'

We became closer friends, trying to understand why A. had been killed. What had he been doing at the time of his death, and who would want him extinguished?

Steve wanted to go back to Syria, even though he told me he believed he was on a blacklist, and that the rebels were after him for something he had written, which he said was not true.

He wrote to me from Michigan, where he was giving a talk on Libya 'to some Texan oil men', to say that he was drifting a bit, going to see his family in Miami, then heading back to covering the war. He wrote to me on Facebook: 'I want to turn my full attention to Syria. I should be in Antakya in early April. I plan to be in that area through summer. I'm starting to look into Raqqa[15]/Hasaka as well as northern Hama and Homs . . . I'd be interested in working on the rape issue with you . . . although as you say, men don't get much from the locals on this topic.'

By 16 April, he said he was 'back on the radar' and preparing to go to Syrian Kurdistan. He still wanted to work on the sexual violence project I was completing. He was having money issues, and sometimes feeling spooked by the enormity of travelling alone, without financial and emotional backing. He was also aware that he was on a sort of list: 'apparently the border idiots have me and Barak on a list and I'm trying to find out how/why . . .'

Do those guys really matter? I asked.

'When I'm being accused of responsibility for the Dir Shifa bombing,[16] I think it does,' he responded tersely. 'Even though I did not enter Syria until weeks after that.'

So don't go, I said. Sounds like the fog of war.

'Sounds like the fog of bullshit,' he replied.

He was not frightened though, or if he was, he did not show it.

'We are all naïve,' he wrote to me shortly after another friend of ours was killed in Aleppo in March 2013. 'I still run out to take video on my cell phone when bombs drop out of jets. It's easy to feel invincible, even with death all around. It's like *This is my movie, Sucker – I'm not going to die!* . . . and on a lighter note, where did you get those food packets when I saw you at Abdullah's. They looked so good behind that aluminum foil in Abdullah's kitchen I seriously almost jacked that shit!'

He returned to the region and on 25 July, he wrote excitedly: 'Hey Mama G! I'm back in Turkey! Have you gotten over your sickness of Aleppo? I may head in early next week.'

He wanted me to meet him and split the costs inside the country. But something that summer made me not want to return to Aleppo. My son was growing too fast, I had already missed too much of his boyhood. I told Steve to be safe, that I wanted to be with my little boy in the summer, that I would come in the autumn and meet him.

'You 2 have fun,' Steve wrote to me, recommending films and ice cream. The last time he wrote to me was a few days before he went missing.

More people were being kidnapped. On another trip, I met a young American girl called Kayla Mueller who had just arrived from Arizona and had come to work with Syrian children. She was with a Syrian friend of mine; she said he was her fiancé. She seemed bubbly and young, naïve and sweet. The challenge of working with Syrian refugees seemed a prospect she was willing to take on, although I could not get an answer from her about who she was working with. A few days later, she would also be kidnapped.

She was twenty-six years old at the time of her death, during a bombing raid in Raqqa, where the Islamic State held her. She never married my friend, and she never had children. She barely got to work with the refugees she wanted to save.

On 6 August 2013, at 2.14 p.m., I got a message from Steve's Facebook account, written by his friend Barak. *Hi Janine. It's Steve's friend Barak. Steve went into Syria 48 hours ago with Yusuf friend of Abdallah and has gone dark. There are rumors on S-Logistics[17] that Yusuf is missing. Do you have contact information for any of his friends inside? Please don't share this information with anyone because no one knows yet.*[18]

We soon found out Steve had been kidnapped and sold to Islamic State. He was held in prison for a year. His family kept it quiet, worried that the kidnappers would realize he was Jewish and that he had studied in Israel, even though he did not hold beliefs that were in line with that state's current government. He shared a cell with other Europeans who were kidnapped, including Jim Foley. He and Jim bonded with the others, sometimes fought, sometimes cried, and then, painfully, watched the others be released as their governments paid a ransom. Steve and Jim must have known – realizing that it was US policy not to pay terrorists – that they would not be released.

In September 2014, Steve Sotloff was murdered, by the 'bearded guys' of the Islamic State, as he had once described them to me. I could not imagine that this smiling, laughing boy, who told jokes and avidly followed the basketball scores of the Miami team he loved, who wrote wise and funny emails, who had offered advice on raising a boy, and who was a generous colleague and friend, had been beheaded.

Jim Foley, too, despite Nicole's desperate search, despite his family's constant interventions, had been beheaded a few weeks before.

I did not, could not, watch the video of either of their murders. But I did see a still photograph of Steve before he was killed, wearing an orange jumpsuit. He had lost weight, a lot of it. His face was no longer chubby and round, and he was not wearing glasses. A random thought crossed my mind: Steve had joked that in Turkey he could not seem to get girls because of his jihadi beard.

Now, his face was clean. There seemed to be no curiosity or youth left in it, just fatigue, an eternal tiredness. He was kneeling in the Syrian desert, looking young, small and weak.

He died brutally in a foreign land, unique in its beauty, surrounded by strangers.

Nicole and I went back to Aleppo in the spring, and this time we stayed with a group of young fighters who were growing more and more radical, more and more Islamic. Now the streets were no longer safe to walk on: as foreigners, we were targets. Now we had to stay in the bedroom assigned to us to eat, where a neighbour woman still left food outside our door on a tray; we weren't allowed in the main room where the men gathered, talking and working on their computers. When we passed to use the bathroom, to wash, to get water from the kitchen, they stopped talking and dropped their eyes.

Aleppo had changed radically, in just a few months. This is when we knew that in desperation, the soldiers who were once fighting for freedom were now radicalized. On the drive out, passing along the road, I tried to look for signs of the old Syria, the one that was there before the Islamists arrived, and did my best to take photographs inside my head, pictures that I would remember, that would show a country that no longer existed.

EPILOGUE

November 2016

In the winter and spring of 2013–14, I worked on a project for the UN's refugee agency, UNHCR, in Jordan, Egypt and Lebanon, about Syrian refugee women who were in exile from their country and raising their children alone.

Along with a team of researchers, we met with these women, their children and their extended families, in the tents, shacks, garages, camps, and in some cases apartments, where they lived. The women were alone because their husbands had been killed in the fighting, or were still fighting in Syria, or were lost. Many of them had never made a single decision in their lives; some had never left the house without a male escort. Some had married as young as fourteen years old. Then they were thrust into a world so far removed from the Syrian countryside where they had lived that the transition was unendurable.

As single women, thought to be 'promiscuous', they were sexual prey for other men in the settlements or camps where they were living. Some were afraid to leave their tents, let alone venture into a nearby village to do the shopping in order to feed their children.

I spoke to one woman in a barren, half-constructed tower block in northern Lebanon, who had survived the Houla massacre by hiding her children as the Shabiha rampaged through the village. Her husband had been killed in the fighting earlier on, and she was alone. She closed the windows and kept the kids out of view, and somehow the militiamen passed over her house. When the killing was finally over, she picked up her children and made her way to the Lebanese border.

In Egypt, I met Maria (her name has been changed), who was working with her two small daughters in a refugee centre. Her story was one of unrelenting pain, but also of resilience. She left Homs (and an abusive husband who had turned 'radical' in the time that the FSA was recruiting) and travelled to central Syria. En route, she was pulled off the bus by government troops and threatened with rape. Her daughters watched from the bus window as she pleaded and begged the soldiers not to abuse her.

She got away. She settled in a small town, only to face arrest again. She left in the middle of the night, went to Latakia, and was taken by the police and put in jail. Her daughters and husband (who had caught up with her) went to Egypt. She followed, only to endure his physical and emotional abuse. In an act of pure courage, she and her daughters escaped and made their way to Cairo.

When I met her in Cairo, she sat at a table in the refugee centre where she was trying to teach other Syrian women how to care for themselves in a strange and new world, and she seemed to me the most courageous woman I had ever met.

'You have to try to make yourself happy,' she told me, for starting a new life after a war had cut into her psyche so profoundly.

Eventually, by boat, by car, by bus and by foot, she made her way to Germany with the girls. But she was, she told me, painfully aware that she would probably never go home.

Over the years, I have met hundreds of refugees from different kinds of war and different kinds of conflict and humanitarian disaster. I always have the same questions, though: *What did you take with you? What did you leave behind? What do you miss the most? How will you re-start your life?*

And, more importantly, I want to know why they left. *What was the exact moment, the trigger, when you felt you had to leave your country? At what point was it unbearable? At what point do you say – enough, now I must leave?*

Or if you decide not to leave, what conditions do you choose to stay under?

For ordinary people, war starts with a jolt: one day you are busy with dentist appointments or arranging ballet lessons for your daughter, and then the curtain drops. One moment the daily routine grinds on; ATMs work and mobile phones function. Then, suddenly, everything stops.

Barricades go up. Soldiers are recruited and neighbours work to form their own defences. Ministers are assassinated and the country falls into chaos. Fathers disappear. The banks close and money and culture and life as people knew it vanishes.

During my time in Damascus when I initially started this book, daily life unfolded as it does everywhere else. I attended operas at one of the best opera houses in the Middle East, bacchanalian pool parties on Thursday afternoons, and weddings in which couples married in elaborate Sunni and Shia ceremonies. I watched makeup artists work their magic on actresses' faces for a magazine photo shoot. All of these activities were part of a life that somehow continued as war crept up to Syria's doorstep, but that has faded away, left as memory.

Not far beneath the surface of the festivities, there was a current of tension, a tangible dread that the month-long conflict would soon spill onto the streets of Damascus. People had begun to leave the city when I arrived. There were going-away parties, and embassies were shutting down. The neighbourhoods of Barzeh and al-Midan, where I walked the streets after Friday Prayer, became no-go areas, opposition strongholds. I wonder how many people I saw at the mosque fled Syria, crossing over the border to Lebanon or Turkey.

I know about the velocity of war. In all of the wars I have covered – including in Bosnia, Iraq, Afghanistan, Sierra Leone, Liberia, Chechnya, Somalia, Kosovo, Libya, and more – the moments in which everything changes from normal to extremely abnormal share a similar quality. One evening in Abidjan, Ivory Coast, in 2002, for example, I went to bed after dinner at a lavish Italian restaurant. When I woke up, there was no telephone service and no radio broadcast in the capital; 'rebels' occupied the television station and flares shot through the sky.

In my garden I could smell both the scent of mango trees and the smell of burning homes. My neighbourhood was on fire. The twenty-four-hour gap between peace and wartime gave me enough time to gather my passport, computer and favourite photos and flee to a hotel in the centre of the city. I never returned to my beloved house with the mango trees.

In early April of 1992, a friend in Sarajevo was walking to her job in a bank, in a mini-skirt and heels, when she saw a tank rolling down the street. Shots were fired. My friend crouched, trembling, behind a rubbish bin, her life for ever altered. In a few weeks, she was sending her baby to safety on a bus, in the arms of a stranger, to another country. She would not see him for years.

This is how war starts.

In the summer of 2012, Major General Robert Mood of Norway, the former chief UN monitor in Damascus, told me there is no template for war. But reading dispatches from the village of Tremseh,[19] and seeing the refugees fleeing Homs with mattresses strapped to their car rooftops, the tiny faces of children pressed against the windows, it is hard not to remember the mistakes of the past two decades. Syrians who called themselves Syrians a few years ago were now saying they were Alawites, Christians, Sunnis, Shias, Druze.

All summer long, and into the following winter and spring, there were political wranglings. Russia continued to veto Security Council efforts to sanction and reproach President Bashar al-Assad.

Diplomacy has failed in the past. The UN had stood on the sidelines and watched as genocide unfolded in Bosnia and Rwanda, during which time Kofi Annan was in charge of peacekeeping operations. At the time of this writing, over 20 years after their crimes, Radovan Karadzic, the 'Butcher of Bosnia', has finally been convicted of war crimes in Srebrenica; Ratko Mladic, a former Bosnian Serb military leader accused of war crimes, is still being tried.

Diplomacy is still failing, but this time in Syria. Kofi Annan also served as UN Envoy to Syria, and eventually left his post in August 2012. Lakhdar Brahimi, a seasoned negotiator who had managed to end the war in Lebanon, held the joint role of UN and Arab League Special Envoy. Brahimi, who was seen by many as the salvation of the region, also left in disgust in May 2014.

As I write this, the Italian/Swedish UN veteran Staffan de Mistura is currently negotiating. De Mistura is a humanitarian – his happiest working conditions were in the field in Bosnia or Sudan. He is doing all he can, but all he can is not ending the war.

In every war I have covered, ceasefire is a synonym for buying time to kill more civilians. Or, as my colleague at the BBC Jim Muir put it so brilliantly, 'truces frequently spur the combatants to try to improve their positions on the ground before the whistle blows and hostilities stop'.[20]

In December, after an extended siege and a month of intense fighting, Bashar al-Assad's forces, helped by his Russian-and-Iranian-backed Hezbollah fighters, seized control of the rebel-held eastern half of Aleppo. Considering your political views, Aleppo either "fell" or was "liberated." At any rate, the Assad victory was a humanitarian disaster and a devastating blow to the embattled anti-government rebels. It was also a signal that the international community had failed, at every level, to negotiate or end the suffering by committing to an end of the war. President Obama was on his way out of the Oval Office and had checked out morally, more or less, leaving the fate of the Syrians to the Russians and Turks, who began to plan a "peace" conference in the Kazakh city of Astana in late January 2017. Staffan de Mistura continued to attempt negotiations, rallying the splintered rebel factions to the table, but in fact they had little leverage to negotiate anything – it was clear that, militarily at least, Assad was winning.

Meanwhile, the images of the civilians fleeing East Aleppo on icy roads, headed to Idlib, were reminiscent of something out of *Doctor Zhivago*. As a reporter, watching these images and talking to the last of my contacts in East Aleppo, I had a sinking, lingering feeling that we had failed on every level to prevent a slaughter in Syria. As of January 2017, it is estimated that more than 450,000 people had died. Some sources put the figure even higher. I am not a millennial social media creature, but I wrote on my Twitter account on 13 December 2016: *Today I feel like a failure. Nearly 25 years reporting war crimes has added up to nothing. We said "never again." What happened? #Aleppo*

Fifteen years ago, Kofi Annan issued a report to the UN General Assembly on the failure of the international community to prevent the massacre of Bosnians at Srebrenica. He called it 'a horror without parallel in the history of Europe since the Second World War'.

Yet once again, the member states lack the will or impetus to stop the slaughter of women and children. As they bicker and squabble over reports and sit in hotel rooms, unable to be the eyes and ears on the ground and report what is happening, more people die.

This is what the beginning of civil war looks like.

In the time I spent in Syria, I talked to as many people as I could, from as many denominations and backgrounds as possible. I wanted to see how Assad's supporters told the story of what was happening to their country. And I wanted testimonies from those who suffered under the regime.

In 2012, before the ceasefire, on the two-hour drive from Damascus to Homs, I went through eight government check-points. Inside Homs, the half of the city that had not been levelled by tanks and fighting was only semi-functioning: the shrubbery in the centre of the road had been left to run wild, but a bus passed through to collect a few lingering people. It was a strange sign of normality.

At a crowded refugee centre, I met a woman named Sopia, who last saw her twenty-three-year-old son, Muhammad, in a Homs hospital bed in December. She told me that shrapnel had hit him during a mortar attack and a piece had lodged in his brain. Sopia said she arrived at his bed one morning and found it empty. Doctors explained to her that they had moved him to a military hospital. Sopia said she had a 'terrible feeling' as she began to search desperately for her son.

She found Muhammad's body, ten days later, in the military hospital. It bore clear signs of torture: there were two bullets lodged in his head, electrocution marks on the soles of his feet and around his ankles and cigarette burns on his back.

For Sopia, the morning she saw her son's body was the moment she realized she was in a country at war. She told me her son was a simple man, a construction worker, and had no links to the rebels. But Sopia and her family lived in Baba Amr – an area of Homs that had been an opposition stronghold – and men of a certain age are assumed to be fighters or supporters of the Free Syrian Army.

I asked Sopia over and over whether her son was a fighter. No, she said, he wasn't.

Sopia's grief was not unlike that of the mothers of government fighters, about the same age as Muhammad, who had been killed in Damascus by IEDs or flying shrapnel. To them and to Sopia, politics matter less than raw pain, inconsolable loss.

That day, which is now fading from my memory, armed soldiers at roadblocks throughout the country checked passing cars for guns and soldiers. Suspicious passengers were detained for questioning. On my way to Homs, polite but menacing pro-Assad gunmen detained me. Sometimes those situations have a silver lining – you are concerned that you might be thrown in jail, but you get to hear people talk about a different vision, a different side. I always listen to them, no matter how abstract their arguments may seem.

In Homs on that trip, I met a little boy who sat on a parquet floor playing Go Fish. For him, the war had started when Syria's Arab Spring began, in March of 2011. Then, his parents forbade him to leave the house. When I visited him, there was a sniper at the end of his street, and in the evening mortar rounds thundered in the dark, and got louder as night wore on.

The little boy lived near the ghostly ruins of Baba Amr, where the air outside his balcony was still rich with the scent of jasmine, olive trees and orange blossoms. If he went inside and closed his eyes, it would be possible for him to believe no war was going on outside.

The boy's family did not support Assad; in fact, the boy's grandmother vehemently loathed him. But they did not leave. Why? The boy's mother told me they were staying because this was their home. Life here was already like life in a prison, a sense that would only worsen.

★ ★ ★

In a government office near the Mezzeh Highway, a Christian official with a Muslim name told me he grew up in a country that, like Bosnia, was a melting pot for ethnic groups, for refugees from Armenia, for Christians, Shias, Sunnis and Greek Orthodox. He said the uprising would change all of this. 'Everyone who believed in the Syrian model is betrayed,' he said.

Now it was June 2014. I was in Baghdad. The border between Syria and Iraq had been erased.

The Islamic State (ISIS) was racing through Iraq, swallowing up entire Yazidi and Christian villages, engulfing anyone who did not embrace its strict Salafist ways.

The Yazidis, a mystical sect, were once again driven out, seeking refuge on a mountain near Sinjar, facing scorching temperatures by day and a lack of water, food and medical care. They were eventually rescued and brought to refugee camps, but ISIS – at the time of this writing – controlled many of the areas where they used to live. UN investigators have accused ISIS forces of genocide and other war crimes in their continuing violence against the ethnic group. Scores of mass graves of Yazidis, especially men and boys who refused to convert to Islam, have been found in the areas that have so far been retaken from ISIS. The Yazidis, whom I visited in 2003 and lived with for several days, attending their weddings and funerals and learning some of the secrets of their faith, had become refugees and wanderers, as they had feared.

A few days after ISIS gained control of Mosul in June 2014, raiding the Central Bank, driving out families and destroying all religious idolatry and statues of poets, I lay on my bed in my hotel in Baghdad, trying to organize my memories in the way that Iraqis do when they are talking about the past. I felt an overriding emotion that entire swathes of the map of the Middle East had been lost. I kept feeling a dull, unending sense of depletion, damage, injury.

As I write this, a coalition force of Iraqi security personnel, Kurdish Peshmerga fighters, Sunni Arab tribesmen, and Shia paramilitary forces, numbering approximately 50,000 in total, have been leading an assault on Mosul since October 2016. On 1 November, the forces had arrived at the eastern edges of Mosul but met heavy fire from the thousands of ISIS fighters in the city. By mid-January 2017, the Iraqi army said it was preparing military operations to retake the part of western Mosul, the last urban stronghold, after capturing most of the eastern part of the city.

My Iraqi friends always refer to epochs: this was back in the Saddam days; that was when I fought in the Iran–Iraq War; this was during the first Gulf War; this was the second invasion; this was after the Americans came. Now it was: before Mosul fell. Now it was: before the war in Syria, before the Arab Spring.

Sometimes, in war, there are also pleasant memories. The camaraderie that exists, the intimacy between human beings, the fact that sometimes barriers are broken down and a level of communication occurs that could never thrive in peacetime. People say things and do things that are profound and genuine.

I remember a hot summer day, in the old town of Damascus, when a famous artist sat in his studio – a room in the former home of a Jewish family who had used it to keep their sacred

Torah – and said the war was edging closer. He was neither pro-government nor pro-opposition; of course he believed in democracy and freedom of expression, being an artist – but most of all he cared simply about creating art.

In 2010, before the Arab Spring, the artist expressed his vision of the future of the Middle East in a sculpture exhibition called *Guillotine*. He opened it first in downtown Damascus.

Now, several years on and with hundreds of thousands dead, something has changed irrevocably in his country. It will not return to what it was, not now, not ever. How can Syria ever be what it once was? It has been burnt alive by hatred.

Shortly before I finished this book in the spring of 2015, after numerous trips back to the region, as ISIS spread past Mosul and reached Palmyra, I got an email from a group of reporters and photographers I had worked with in Sarajevo during the Bosnian war. They had put together a collection of photographs and writing, our memories, into a time module, a way of not letting anyone forget, ever, what happened to that defeated and broken country.

They had bundled our words and photographs and some haunting music together to make a ten-minute presentation that basically traced the war from beginning to end – from the first nationalist parades, to the murders of innocents, to the mass graves and the destruction of mosques, villages and cities, and finally to the Dayton Agreement in 1995, which ended the war. It was our way of saying: look, this is how war begins, how it destroys, how it ultimately ends. Nothing good comes from it.

I could not help watching the short film over and over, the way you pick at a wound that hurts, and the more you pick, the more painful and sore it grows, but you continue. And every time I watched it, tears rolled down my face onto my T-shirt, just as they had that day in the hospital in Aleppo. I felt ashamed of my reaction – after all, I had survived, I had not been ethnically cleansed from my village or been raped or had my parents murdered in front of me – but most of all I felt immense sorrow. We had tried, my colleagues and I and dedicated humanitarians and diplomats, but we had failed to protect the very people we had come to report on, to stop the killing, to somehow not allow this country to be ripped apart, limb from limb – and, in the words of the poet Anne Sexton – throat, eye, knucklebone.[21]

I swore to myself, after Bosnia, that I would never live through another war that would consume me. I swore that I would not feel again the terrible stirring of guilt so profound – that feeling of *we did nothing*. I wondered sometimes what my life would be like had I never stumbled into a war zone for the first time when I was a very young woman, so young that I was embarrassed to tell my age.

How different my life would have been had I never seen a mass grave or a truck with bodies, all dead, piled one on top of the other, their skin changing from the softness of the living to the leathery skin of the dead. Or a torture cell with the incarcerated's dying wish and last words of love to his family.

But that is not what happens. In an unexpected reversal, the Syrian government recently granted me a visa for Damascus. As I prepare to return to this country that has seen unimaginable violence since I last went, I think of Charles Tilly, the political scientist I studied so diligently as a student, and his theory that men are inevitably linked to war as a way of state-making. Wars make states — or is it the other way around? Do states make wars?

I have never been very good at theory. But I am good at counting, and attempting to remember those who lived, who walked the earth, but who fell during the course of the violence that ripped their countries apart.

As I write this, the Syrian war continues and there are over 400,000 Syrians dead. The Book of the Dead is not yet finished.

Notes

1   According to the Human Rights Watch, the Bosnian genocide between 1992 and 1995 resulted in an estimated 100,000 deaths of Bosniak Muslims and Croatians by Serb forces; it was the worst act of genocide since the Nazi regime's destruction. While the UN did little to prevent the systematic atrocities committed against Bosniaks and Croats in Bosnia while they were occurring, it did actively seek justice against those who committed them. In May 1993, the UN Security Council created the International Criminal Tribunal for the Former Yugoslavia (ICTY) at The Hague, Netherlands. It was the first international tribunal since the Nuremberg Trials in 1945–46 and the first to prosecute genocide, among other war crimes. In the weeks after 6 April 1994, 800,000 men, women and children perished in the Rwandan genocide, perhaps as many as three-quarters of the Tutsi population. Tens of thousands of Tamils were murdered in Sri Lanka during a twenty-five-year war. In both these genocides, the international community failed to intervene in a timely or effective manner. Despite a UN mission in Kosovo, human trafficking continues, as does rape in the Congo, which is perpetrated mostly by the Congolese forces. Five years after the Haitian earthquake, Haiti suffers from disease and poverty, unable to develop a stable government amidst the international NGOs. Sometimes absent and sometimes present too late, the United Nations seems unable to resolve these issues, despite the sincere determination of some of its officials.

2   Freeze zones are meant to suspend fighting in some areas and allow humanitarian aid to be delivered. 'It should be something that freezes the conflict in that area and gives an opportunity for some type of humanitarian improvement and for the people to feel that,

at least there, there will not be this type of conflict,' de Mistura said (al-Arabiya News). It is an 'action plan' rather than a 'peace plan'.

3 From *4th Report of the Commission of Enquiry on the Syrian Arab Republic*, A/HRC/22/59 (5 Feburary 2013), by United Nations, General Assembly. © United Nations 2013. Reprinted with the permission of the United Nations.

4 A United Nations report in August 2012 into an earlier massacre at Houla found that the indiscriminate attacks against civilian populations and other atrocities were 'state policy' and claimed Assad's forces and allied Shabiha militia were involved at the highest levels in 'gross violations of international human rights'.

The UN inquiry found that anti-Assad forces had also committed war crimes including 'murder, extrajudicial execution and torture', but that these abuses 'did not reach the gravity, frequency and scale of those committed by government forces and the Shabiha'.

The 102-page report said that Syrian government forces and Shabiha fighters have carried out numerous war crimes in the country including murder, torture and the massacre of 100 civilians, almost half of them children, near the town of Houla in May, 2012. The UN's independent international commission of inquiry said the violations were the result of 'state policy'. It claimed President Bashar al-Assad's 'security forces and government' at the highest levels were involved in 'gross violation of international human rights'. The violations included 'unlawful killing, indiscriminate attacks against civilian populations and acts of sexual violence', it said. The report painted a bleak picture of events on the ground in Syria, noting the situation inside the country had 'deteriorated significantly' since February.

The commission, led by investigator Paulo Pinheiro, also reported that Syria's rebels were guilty of violations including murder, torture and extra-judicial killings. But it said abuses by anti-government groups were not 'of the same gravity, frequency and scale' as those committed by Syrian regime forces and allied Shabiha militia.

5 Robert Fisk, *Independent*, UK, 29 August 2012: 'Inside Daraya – how a failed prisoner swap turned into a massacre'. © Independent Print Limited, Robert Fisk and *Independent*.

6 The source is a Syrian journalist who wishes to remain anonymous.

7 Hugh Macleod, *Global Post*, 26 August 2012, 'Inside Syria: For assault on Daraya, Assad regime brings own cameras' http://www.globalpost.com/dispatch/news/regions/middle-east/syria/120826/inside-syria-sunday-massacre-daraya-assad-regime-brin?page=0,1

8 Abeer Al-Ahmad, https://wikileaks.org/plusd/cables/08DAMASCUS445_a.html

9 These words are from the same journalist as mentioned in note 6 above, who wishes to remain anonymous for safety reasons.

10 See this link for a video of barrel bombing of Darayya, but please note, the content is disturbing. http://www.telegraph.co.uk/news/worldnews/middleeast/syria/10618670/Syrian-military-drop-devastating-barrel-bombs-on-city.html

11 The United States Armed Forces' term for urban warfare is UO, an abbreviation for Urban Operations. The previously used US military term, MOUT, an abbreviation for Military Operations in Urban Terrain, has been replaced by UO, although the term MOUT is still in use.

The British Armed Forces' terms are OBUA (Operations in Built-Up Areas), FIBUA (Fighting In Built-Up Areas), or sometimes (colloquially) FISH (Fighting In Someone's House), or FISH and CHIPS (Fighting In Someone's House and Causing Havoc In People's Streets). The term FOFO (Fighting In Fortified Objectives) refers to clearing enemy personnel from narrow and entrenched places like bunkers, trenches and strongholds; the dismantling of mines and wires; and the securing of footholds in enemy areas. For more historic essays on the subject, see *Military Operations in Built-Up Areas: X. Essays on Some Past, Present, and Future Aspects*, Lilita I. Dzirkals, Konrad Kellen and Horst Mendershausen, Rand Corporation, 1976.

12 In both Aleppo and Daraa, Human Rights Watch documented repeated barrel-bomb attacks since the passage of Security Council Resolution 2139 on 22 February 2014, striking near or on medical facilities, and in residential areas with schools, mosques and markets, and without discernible military targets in the vicinity. Barrel bombs are unguided high explosive weapons that are cheaply made, locally produced and typically constructed from large oil drums, gas cylinders and water tanks, filled with high explosives and scrap metal to enhance fragmentation, and then dropped from helicopters usually flying at high altitude.

13 Human Rights Watch. 'Syria: Barrage of Barrel Bombs', 30 July 2014. © Human Rights Watch 2014.

14 http://en.qantara.de/content/destruction-of-historic-sites-syria-is-losing-its-history

15 Raqqa would become the capital of the so-called Islamic State in 2014.

16 Dir Shifa was a hospital in Aleppo that was bombed and destroyed by the Syrian Army in November 2012. This left the local population – quite rightly – distraught, suspicious of all foreigners and angry.

17 Private Facebook page for journalists and aid workers inside Syria.

18 Private correspondence between the author and Steven Sotloff.

19 The battle of Tremseh, a village twenty-two miles northeast of Hama, took place in the late hours of 12 July 2012. The Syrian Army was fighting the Free Syrian Army. Initially, there were reports of a massacre, with dozens if not hundreds killed, including civilians. But two days later, the UN observer mission issued a statement, based on an investigation by a UN team that went to the town, reporting that the Syrian Army had mainly targeted the homes of rebels and activists. The BBC later reported this was a 'contradiction of the initial opposition claims of a civilian massacre'. The number of civilian casualties was unclear. The village was primarily inhabited by Sunni Muslims.

20 http://www.bbc.com/news/world-middle-east-31514447?fb_ref=Default

21 'And what of the dead? They lie without shoes in their stone boats. They are more like stone than the sea would be if it stopped. They refuse to be blessed, throat, eye and knucklebone.' Anne Sexton, 'The Truth the Dead Know'.

Acknowledgements

So many people helped this book come to light that I will try to start at the beginning . . .

First, my thanks to the Syrian people, my friends who cannot be named, and those I do not know, for their courage and fortitude in the face of such a brutal war.

My publishers, Alexandra Pringle at Bloomsbury and Phil Marino at Norton, who waited, encouraged and believed enough in a book about war, and the late Ash Green at Knopf, who found and shaped me as a very young writer.

Lara Adoumie, a junior at Bowdoin College with a Syrian dad, who worked tirelessly and consistently on the final drafts, checking, editing and formatting. Yemile Bucay, another intern of Syrian/Mexican origin, who added her expertise on international relations and history, and Fredrik Elisson – my brilliant intern.

My dear friend Christopher Silvester, who helped me with the copy editing, and Honey Al Sayed, a Syrian reporter now living in America because she cannot live in her own country, who acted as one of my first readers.

Darren Dale 'Chalkie' White, who kept me alive and safe on many a voyage, talking me down when I was terrified; he literally gave me directions on where to go to crawl under a fence to get out of Syria and reach Turkey safely.

Fred Pakis, who gave me the opportunity to earn an MA in International Relations at the Fletcher School of Diplomacy, Tufts University. Mr Pakis awarded me a full scholarship so that I could put my reporting skills into an academic and diplomatic framework. Words cannot express my gratitude for the extraordinary gift of knowledge that he has given me.

My agents, Kim Witherspoon; David Forrer; William Callahan; David Godwin. At Bloomsbury, Angelique Tran Van Sang, Catherine Best and Steve Cox.

A special thank you to The Investigative Fund at The Nation Institute, and Esther Kaplan, who gave me two grants to help research this book. Mark Gevisser, for introducing me to Esther. Robert Templer at The Center for Conflict, Negotiation and Recovery, Central European University, who gave me the role of Senior Policy Adviser, a chance to delve deeper into Aleppo. Kim Abbot, then at International Crisis Group, whom I had never met, but who reached out to help a sister make connections and contacts. Karmen and Carne Ross, for their inspiration of tirelessly trying to make the world a better place,

At *Granta* magazine, who first commissioned me to write about Syria, I want to thank John Freeman, Ellah Allfrey, Sigrid Rausing, Emily Greenhouse, Saskia Vogel and Yuka Igarashi for their support and their commitment to publishing long-format literary non-fiction. Ellen Rosenbush at *Harper's*, for your friendship on Dark Stormy Nights in Brooklyn. At the *Guardian*, Clare Longrigg and Jonathan Shahin.

My editors and colleagues at *Newsweek* who were unspeakably patient with my insistence on writing about Syria and ISIS: Johnathan Davis; Etienne Uzac; James

Impoco; Kira Bindrim; Claudia Parsons; Mikka Schaller; Nicholas Wapshott; Annette Fetzer; Balbina Calo; Abigail Jones; Leah McGrath Goodman; Damien Sharkov; Richard Addis; Victor Sebestyen; Cordelia Jenkins.

At *Vanity Fair*, Bruce Handy, Graydon Carter and David Friend.

In Syria: Nicole Tung; Paddy Wells; Scott Rosenfeld; Robert Rippberger; Clare Morgana Gillis; Nir Rosen; Nada Kettunen; Kate Brooks; Renata Dwan; Georgette Gagnon; Elio Tamburi Qunteiro; Omar K.; Liz Sly; Leena Saidi; Lina Khitab; Fadi Dayoub; Ghid Zraik; Joelle Eid; Juliette Touma; Khaled; Dr Luna al Sham; Mouhamad Diab; Nadia Abu Amr; Noura al Yafi; Rafif; Sajad Jiyad; Shoueb Rifai; Kinan Madi; Suzan Haidamous; Waddah abd Rabbo; Yara Bader; Abdi Nova; Yassir the 47th; Catherine Philp; Martin Chulov; Leena Saidi; Liz Sly; Faris S. and Wael.

Dr Annie Sparrow; Peter Harland; Robert Danin; Paul Wood; Ruth Sherlock; Anne Bernard; Suzan Alandry; Peter Bergen; Andrew Gilmour who gave professional support.

And all the brave activists.

In Iraq: Ahmed Chalabi; Tamara Chalabi; Zaab Sethna; Ali Almalawi; Ali al-Saffar; Haider Kata; Sajad Jiyad; Shadi Hamid; Mohamad Rasoul; Ali Hussein; Binar Faeq Karim; Borzou Datagahi; Dr Mowaffak al Rubaie; Hala Gorani; Fareed Yasin; Hanaa Edwar; Jonathan Cohen; Justin Theron; Louay al-Khattib; Sam Morris; Mais Albayaa; Peyman Pejman; Tim Spicer; Robin Gwinner; William Warda; Alice Walpole.

Mona Mahmoud – who shared so much with me, sorrow and joy.

ACKNOWLEDGEMENTS

At UNHCR: Melissa Fleming; Edith Champagne; Sybella Wilkes; Clare Gillis; Rose Foran; Nadia abu Amr; Rebecca Dowd; Lynsey Addario; Mimi Little-Boyer.

At Reid Hall, and Sciences Po, Paris: Lisa Fleury; Marianne 'Nari' Fischer; Ali Shajrawi; Sophie Zinser; Tess Morgan; Sarah-Nicole LeFlore; Medina Adlova; Kyle Waggoner; Rose Foran.

The teams at Human Rights Watch and Amnesty International have consistently aided me with my work over the past two decades, and have been a shining example to me of courage and persistence: Emma Daly; Peter Bouekart; Anna Neistat; Ole Solvang; Erin Evins; Donatella Rovera; Steve Cranshaw; Sevag Kechichian; Ken Roth; Adam Coogle; Liesl Gernholtz; Lama Fakih; Tom Porteous; Corinne Dufka; Priyanka Motaparthy.

At the *New York Times* I should like to thank Michael Slackman, Cynthia Latimer, Kyle Crichton, Susan Lehman, Mark Thompson and Joe Kahn.

My tribe: Ariane Quentier; Mariann Wenckheim; Alba Arikha; Christopher Silvester; Stelios Kalamotusis; Charlotte Fraser; Catherine Rubin Kermogant; Kati Marton; Mimi and Max Mulhern; Anna Sessau; John Harrison; Susan Steele; Robert Pay; Susannah and Tonio Weiss; Leslie Camhi; Bettina von Hase; Gloria Orrigi; Adam Phillips; Wendell Steavenson.

Special thanks to my web designer and sister, Isabel Villavechia. And much love to AJ and Holly, and Baroness Arminka Helic.

Bénédicte de Roquefeuil and Diana de Gunzburg offered me their beautiful homes in Brittany and Normandy to write. Ashley and Cuotie Malle let me lie on a hammock in

181

Provence and do nothing but read and think before another worrying trip to the region, alone. Thank you.

The GMAP team at Fletcher School of Law and Diplomacy – my classmates and professors, who inspired me with their brilliance. Special thanks to Dean Deborah Nutter and Mariana Stoyancheva. Mohamedou Mahmoud and Ambassador Christian Dussey at the Geneva Center for Security Policy for the Fellowship.

Bruce Shapiro, Frank Ochberg and all my fellow Ochberg Fellows 2015 at the Dart Center, Columbia University, who gave me the chance to examine war and trauma on a deeper level.

The Syria negotiators, Staffan de Mistura and Lakhdar Brahimi, who gave me their time and wisdom, and also listened to my own thoughts on Syria. Michael Contet, at the Office of the Special Envoy for Syria, was an efficient and capable facilitator. Juliette Touma was always generous with her time.

At home, my son Luca Costantino Girodon – my heart's treasure – and his father, Bruno Girodon, who put up with my many voyages. My mother, Kathryn di Giovanni, who worried about me all the time, but knew better than to say anything. My sister Judith and my niece Janine Cifaretto for their friendship. My godchildren, Carter Spyrka and Deni Jokic. My brothers, Robert and Vincent. And Constance Griffin, my true heart.

And thanks to LR, who inspired me to start this project in 2011, and gave support along the way.

And to the memory of my colleagues, Steve Sotloff; Jim Foley; Marie Colvin. And my late brothers, Richard and Joseph di Giovanni. I miss you every single day.

Chronology

Early History: Warring Empires

3rd millennium BC–539 BC	The area that is modern-day Syria was occupied successively by Sumerians, Egyptians, Hittites, Assyrians and Babylonians. The Assyrian Empire rose to supremacy in the 15th century BC and ruled for almost a thousand years.
539–64 BC	The Persians, Alexander the Great and the Seleucid Empire ruled parts of Syria as part of their empires.
64 BC–6th century AD	Roman General Pompey the Great captured Antioch and turned Syria into a Roman province. Its prosperity made it one of the most important parts of the empire. After the decline of Rome, Syria became part of the East Roman or Byzantine Empire.
7th century AD	Muslim Arabs, led by Khalid ibn al-Walid, conquered Syria, which became part of the Islamic Empire. The Umayyad dynasty, then rulers of the Islamic Empire, placed the capital of the empire in Damascus, and divided Syria into four districts: Damascus, Homs, Palestine and Jordan. There was toleration of Christians in this era and several held government posts.
750–969	The Umayyad dynasty was overthrown by the Abbasid dynasty, which moved the capital to Baghdad. In the Ikhshidid Empire, the court of Ali Saif al-Daula was a centre of culture, thanks to its nurturing of Arabic literature.
969–1516	Syria was occupied by invading waves of Byzantines, Turks, Egyptians and briefly Mongols. The Christian population suffered persecution.
1516–1918	The Ottoman Empire conquered Syria after defeating the Mamluks near Aleppo, and Syria became part of the Ottoman Empire, reorganized into one large province.

20th Century: Consolidation of the Syrian Nation

1916–18   During the First World War, in the Sykes-Picot Agreement, the British and French secretly agreed on the post-war division of the Ottoman Empire into respective zones of influence. In 1918 Arab and British troops advanced into Syria and captured Damascus and Aleppo. Syria became a League of Nations mandate under French control (with Lebanon). The country was divided into three autonomous regions by the French, with separate areas for the Alawites on the coast and the Druze in the south.

1925–7   Great Syrian Revolt. Led by Sultan al-Atrash in the Druze Mountains, the nationalist movement spread across the whole of Syria and parts of Lebanon. The revolt saw fierce battles between rebel and French forces in Damascus, Homs and Hama.

1936–46   Syria and France negotiated a treaty of independence; France agreed to Syrian independence in principle, but maintained French military and economic dominance. During the Second World War, Syria came under the control of Vichy France, but in 1941 British and Free French Forces occupied the country in the Syria-Lebanon campaign in July. Syrian independence was declared, but not immediately ratified. Finally in 1946 the Syrian Arab Republic was officially recognized as an independent republic.

1946–58   Skirmishes with Israel, then newly established, frequent changes of government and coups d'état finally ended with a merging of Egypt and Syria in 1958 under the title of United Arab Republic.

1961–70   Syria re-established independence from Egypt in 1961. Rival elements of the Ba'ath party fought for supremacy until Hafez al-Assad, in a bloodless coup, took control in 1970 and began the Assad family's domination of Syria. At this point a new Syrian constitution was drafted and ratified under the strong guidance of the new president, defining Syria as a secular socialist state with Islam recognized as the majority religion, and asserting that freedom is a sacred right and democracy is the ideal form of government.

1973–81   Syria and Egypt initiated the Yom Kippur War by launching a surprise attack on Israel, reigniting years of conflict. Syrian troops also intervened in Lebanon's civil war in 1976 and remained there for 30 years.

1982–94   Syrian troops continued to occupy Lebanon and to carry out skirmishes with Israel. In 1994 the Assad dynasty was thrown into chaos when Hafez al-Assad's eldest son, Bassel al-Assad, who had been likely to succeed his father, was killed in a car accident.

CHRONOLOGY

Early 21st Century: Growing Discontent

2000–1	President Hafez al-Assad died in 2000 after 30 years in power. Parliament amended the constitution, reducing the minimum age of the President from 40 years to 34, which allowed Hafez al-Assad's son Bashar to take over, and he became President after a referendum in which he ran unopposed. In November 2000, Assad called for the release of some 600 political prisoners. The 'Damascus Spring' ended in August 2001 with the arrest and imprisonment of leading activists who had called for democratic elections.
2002–5	The United States claimed Damascus was acquiring weapons of mass destruction and included Syria in a list of states that they said made up an 'axis of evil'. The US imposed economic sanctions on Syria over what it called its support for terrorism and failure to stop militants entering Iraq.
2005–10	Renewed opposition activity led to long jail terms for activists. However, diplomatic relations with other countries, including the US, European Union and Iraq, were restored. Discussions were held with Israel regarding a peace treaty, with Turkey as mediator. The bulk of the Syrian forces withdrew from Lebanon.
2010–11	The thaw in diplomatic relations with the West came to an abrupt end as the US renewed sanctions against Syria, saying that it supported terrorist groups, sought weapons of mass destruction and had provided Lebanon's Hezbollah with Scud missiles in violation of UN resolutions.

The Civil War

2011: Protests and Civil Uprising

	Inside Syria	International Reaction
January – **mid-March**	A self-immolation in the north, plus small-scale demonstrations and protests.	
March	A dozen teenagers are violently arrested in Daraa for painting anti-regime graffiti. There are calls for a 'Day of Rage' and 'Day of Dignity'. Mass protests in Damascus and Aleppo soon spread to other cities. Security forces open fire and kill protesters, inciting further unrest. Assad's first speech about the conflict on 30 March blames foreign conspirators.	
April	Protests continue and spread. Assad announces conciliatory measures. On 22 April the 'Great Friday' protest leads to over 100 people killed. Protesters call for the downfall of the regime. The crackdown strengthens. Hundreds are killed as the army launches military attacks on towns and besieges Daraa.	International media begins to refer to the protests as an 'uprising'. The US and France condemn the crackdown and call for reform.
May	The government sends tanks into Homs, Daraa and areas of Damascus. Reports emerge of Iran providing assistance to quell the uprising. There are over 1,100 civilian deaths during the month.	The US imposes sanctions on Assad for human rights abuses. The EU implements an arms embargo, asset freeze and travel ban on senior officials.

	Inside Syria	**International Reaction**
June	50,000 protest in Hama; 34 are killed. Government cuts off internet access. Armed rebellion in the north leaves 120 soldiers dead. More than 10,000 civilians flee from the north to Turkey. Opposition activists establish their own 'National Council'. Assad is still blaming 'foreign conspiracies', 'vandals' and terrorists for the unrest.	The Arab League openly condemns the regime's violent crackdown.
July	Protests continue to increase and spread. Free Syrian Army (FSA) is formed by seven defecting officers. Siege of Hama and 'Ramadan massacre': 136 killed in the bloodiest day of uprising to date. According to a former Assad regime security official, Syrian intelligence agencies deliberately released Islamist militants from prison between July and October to subvert the peaceful uprising and ignite a violent rebellion. The project was overseen by the General Security Directorate, one of the most important and most feared Syrian organizations. Inmates from Saidnaya prison, 50 km north of Damascus, went on to become prominent members of insurgent groups. See *The National*, 21 January 2014.	US Secretary of State Hillary Clinton condemns the regime. US says Assad has lost his legitimacy.

	Inside Syria	International Reaction
August	Formation of the Syrian National Council in Istanbul, a coalition of groups opposed to Assad based outside and within the country. This later becomes part of the Syrian National Coalition.	Saudi Arabia, Bahrain and Kuwait recall their ambassadors. The UK, US, EU and others demand that Assad steps down. US bans oil imports from Syria. The UN condemns human rights violations and the use of force against civilians.
September		The EU bans oil imports from Syria. Ambassadors from US, EU, UK, Japan and Canada take part in a vigil supporting the protests. Turkey, Assad's former ally, cuts contact with Syrian authorities.
October	Siege of Homs. Government troops shell the city.	UN Security Council (UNSC) attempts to pass a resolution condemning Assad's government and issuing sanctions. Russia and China veto it. UN High Commissioner for Human Rights, Navi Pillay, says the crisis shows signs of 'descending into an armed struggle'.
November	FSA attacks a military base near Damascus in the highest-profile assault yet. Pro-government Syrians attack foreign embassies.	Arab League votes to suspend Syria if it does not adhere to peace plan. It imposes harsh sanctions on Assad regime. Jordan's King Abdullah calls on Assad to step down.
December	Security forces fire on an anti-government demonstration in Hama. 200 are reportedly massacred in Idlib. UN reports that over 5,000 have been killed since the outbreak of the conflict. Over 500,000 people protest across the country.	Syria agrees to admit Arab League observers to monitor compliance with an agreement by which the government pledges to pull troops and heavy weapons out of civilian areas and allow access to journalists and human rights workers.

2012: Armed Insurgency and Escalation

	Inside Syria	International Reaction
January	Jabhat al-Nusra is formed as Syria's al-Qaeda affiliate. This is initially effective against the regime and an ally of more moderate groups.	Arab League calls for Assad to step down and withdraws observers owing to violence.
February	Two car bombs in Aleppo kill 28. Government steps up bombardment of Homs and other cities. Hundreds die. Al-Qaeda head Ayman al-Zawahiri calls for militants across the region to fight Assad. Government-controlled areas vote on a new constitution establishing multi-party system. The polls are widely derided as a sham.	UNSC tables resolution to support Arab League plan. Russia and China veto it. US closes its embassy. UN condemns human rights violations and demands Assad's resignation. Kofi Annan is appointed Joint Special Envoy of the UN and Arab League.
March	FSA retreats from Baba Amr in Homs citing concerns for civilian welfare and inability to defend it against better-armed troops. Syrian troops retake the district.	Six Gulf states close their embassies. UNSC, including Russia and China, endorses non-binding peace plan. It fails and fighting continues.
April	Assad claims to have regained control over the country. Rebels accuse government troops of continued massacres.	UN brokers a ceasefire and observers are deployed. International Friends of Syria coalition convenes in Istanbul and votes to recognize Syrian National Council. US and Arab states promise to aid rebels.
May	Security forces raid Aleppo University. More people are killed here and in Damascus. Parliamentary elections are held but boycotted by opposition. 108 people including 49 children killed in Houla.	UN Human Rights Council accuses Assad's troops of war crimes. France, UK, Germany, Italy, Spain, Canada and Australia expel senior Syrian diplomats in protest at killing of civilians in Houla.

	Inside Syria	International Reaction
June	UN observers fired on while trying to reach Haffa. They are met with the 'stench of death'. Russia sends two warships to Syria to protect its base. Turkey changes rules of engagement after Syria shoots down a Turkish plane. This prompts an emergency NATO meeting.	UN Under-Secretary for Peacekeeping Operations, Hervé Ladsous, calls the conflict 'full-scale civil war'. UN suspends observer patrols. Geneva I talks held, resulting in Geneva communiqué.
July	200 massacred in village of Tremseh by government forces. In retaliation FSA bombs National Security building in Damascus, killing top Assad aides, and seizes Aleppo.	UNSC tables a resolution threatening sanctions against Syria; Russia and China veto it. UNHCR refugee camp opened in Jordan. This becomes home to 80,000 displaced Syrians.
August	Security forces kill 400 in Damascus suburb and 40 more in Azaz near the Turkish border.	Kofi Annan resigns and Lakhdar Brahimi takes over as Special Envoy. UN says both government troops and rebels have committed crimes against humanity. Obama states that Assad's use of chemical weapons would be a 'red line' tilting the US towards intervention.
September		US pledges to supply rebels with $45 million of non-lethal aid.
October	Fighting and bomb attacks in various cities. Fire destroys the ancient market in Aleppo. Syrian-Turkish tension rises when Syrian mortar fire kills five civilians in a Turkish border town. Turkey intercepts a Syrian plane allegedly carrying arms from Russia.	

	Inside Syria	International Reaction
November	Rebels shoot down two military aircraft. National Coalition for Syrian Revolutionary and Opposition Forces formed in Qatar, excluding Islamist militias. Israeli military fire on Syrian artillery units across the Golan Heights, the first such return of fire since the Yom Kippur War of 1973.	UN says rebels may have committed war crimes by summarily executing captured soldiers.
December	Rebels gain ground in Damascus, taking a number of military bases and pushing towards the airport. UNHCR confirms more than half a million Syrians have fled the country as refugees.	US, Britain, France, Turkey and Gulf states formally recognize the opposition National Coalition as the 'legitimate representative' of the Syrian people. US labels Jabhat al-Nusra a terrorist organization.

2013: The Rise of Islamic State

	Inside Syria	International Reaction
January	Assad says he will introduce political reforms to end the war but violence continues with bombings in Aleppo and Damascus. 65 people are found executed, bound and shot, in Aleppo. A convoy carrying anti-aircraft weapons is hit by air strikes – Israel is suspected of the attack.	International donors pledge more than $1.5 billion to help Syrian civilians. US says it will give medical supplies and food aid to National Coalition but not military support. US and Russia hold peace plan talks brokered by Brahimi, ending without a breakthrough.
February	Bombing in Damascus kills dozens of Ba'ath party members and others. Rebels continue to make advances with the help of foreign arms.	US and UK once again pledge non-military aid to rebels.

	Inside Syria	International Reaction
March	Syrian planes bomb Raqqa after rebels seize control of the town. Islamists set up the Eastern Council. Reports of Jabhat al-Nusra implementing Islamic Law. Weapons flow in from Iran.	Obama and Putin seek 'New Syria Initiatives' for peaceful resolution to the conflict. EU vetoes Franco-British push to arm Syrian rebels. UN says more than a million Syrians are now refugees. Arab League gives Syria's place to the National Coalition.
April	Foreign jihadis in Syria grow in number with the appearance of Islamic State (ISIS). Its leader Abu Bakr al-Baghdadi announces merger with Jabhat al-Nusra, which is spurned by al-Nusra. Hezbollah leader Hassan Nasrallah says his Shiite fighters are supporting Assad.	UK and France report to UN that chemical weapons have been used by Assad. UNSC reaches agreement on Syria, calling for an end to violence and condemning human rights violations. US pledges additional $23 million in non-lethal aid to rebels.
May	Air strikes hit a shipment of missiles from Iran in Damascus. Car bombings and clashes leave 50 dead in bordering countries. Hezbollah sends thousands of fighters to help Assad.	EU lifts its arms embargo on Syrian opposition but keeps embargo on Assad regime. UN says 4.25 million Syrians are displaced within Syria.
June	Government recaptures the strategically important town of al-Qusair, between Homs and the Lebanese border. Massacre of over 60 in Hatla by rebels. UN says 93,000 have been killed in the conflict so far, revised a few days later to over 100,000.	US says that the Syrian regime has used chemical weapons on several occasions in past 12 months and concludes that direct military support can be provided to rebels. UN calls Syria the 'worst humanitarian disaster' since the Cold War.

	Inside Syria	International Reaction
July	Saudi-backed Ahmed Jarba becomes leader of the National Coalition. Government troops advance in Homs and occupy the Khalid Ibn Al-Walid mosque, a symbol for rebels. The Syrian government begins a siege of Yarmouk Palestinian refugee camp near Damascus, leading to hundreds starving to death. Amnesty condemns the siege as a crime against humanity.	
August	Chemical weapons in a Damascus suburb kill 1,429 people in their sleep. Human Rights Watch (HRW) suspects sarin gas was used. UN weapons inspectors are sent in a few days later and come under fire from snipers.	The use of chemical weapons forces Obama to consider a limited military strike with Congressional backing. UK prime minister David Cameron also calls for a military response but this is rejected in parliament.
September	Eleven of the biggest Islamist rebel groups reject the National Coalition's aims and declare their goal of an Islamic state.	Russia questions US intelligence on the chemical attack and issues a warning over US air strikes. Russia proposes a diplomatic solution with Syria signing the Chemical Weapons Convention. US agrees. UN inspectors declare that they found 'clear and convincing evidence' of sarin gas being used. UN resolution 2118, aiming to eliminate chemical weapons, is adopted unanimously.
October		Inspectors arrive to begin destroying chemical weapons.

	Inside Syria	International Reaction
November	Islamist rebels make gains in Deir Al-Zor province.	
December		2.3 million refugees are confirmed in Turkey, Iraq, Jordan, Lebanon and Egypt, many living in refugee camps. US and Britain suspend any support for rebels after Islamist rebels seize FSA bases. Navi Pillay says UN fact-finding team has amassed evidence of the Syrian government's complicity in war crimes to the 'highest levels'.

2014: Heading for Stalemate

Date	Inside Syria	International Reaction
January	UN temporarily stops reporting death tolls through inability to verify the information. War crimes analysts say smuggled information shows torture and killing of prisoners on an 'industrial scale'.	Geneva II peace talks begin, including US, Russia, Syrian government and the National Coalition. No progress is made.
February	Government barrel bombs kill almost 250 in Aleppo.	Second round of Geneva peace talks fail. US warns the war could become a 'perpetual stalemate'.
March	Syrian Army and Hezbollah recapture the rebel stronghold of Yabroud. Israel launches air strikes on Syrian forces.	

Date	Inside Syria	International Reaction
April	Jordanian Air Force strikes a convoy near the border. Later reports suggest it may have been rebels seeking refuge from government troops.	
May	Rebels are evacuated from Homs, marking the end of three years of resistance in the city. An HRW report claims that Assad's forces have used chlorine gas bombs and barrel bombs on rebel-held areas.	Special Envoy Lakhdar Brahimi resigns and apologizes for the failure of peace talks.
June	General elections in government-held areas. Opposition groups and the international community describe them as a sham. ISIS militants declare a 'caliphate' in territory stretching from Aleppo to the eastern Iraqi province of Diyala.	
July	ISIS consolidates power and takes a large military base near Raqqa.	UNSC votes to allow cross-border aid to victims of the conflict in rebel-held areas. Staffan de Mistura is appointed UN Special Envoy to Syria.
August	ISIS controls the entire Raqqa province. US journalist James Foley is killed by ISIS in the first of a number of gory execution videos.	US assembles an international anti-ISIS coalition in Paris. UN says that ISIS has committed human rights abuses and atrocities.
September	ISIS executes journalist Steven Sotloff. The US and five Arab countries launch air strikes against ISIS around Aleppo and Raqqa. ISIS launches a huge assault on the Kurdish border enclave of Kobani.	Obama authorizes air strikes in Syria against ISIS. Special Envoy Staffan de Mistura visits Damascus.

Date	Inside Syria	International Reaction
October	ISIS advances into Kobani but is pounded by Coalition air strikes. Syrian government forces surround Aleppo, cutting off the main supply lines to the city. Lebanon closes its borders to Syrian refugees after more than a million people flee there to escape the fighting.	Special Envoy de Mistura calls for 'freeze zones' around Aleppo to allow humanitarian aid in.
November	Jabhat al-Nusra pushes the Hazm Movement, an alliance of moderate Syrian rebels, out of Idlib province. The secular militia had been supplied with US weapons.	NGOs say the international community must do more to help civilians fleeing the civil war. Turkey, Iraq, Lebanon and Jordan are being overwhelmed by refugees. Special Envoy Staffan de Mistura visits Damascus again.
December	The Syrian government allows the World Health Organization (WHO) to deliver medical supplies to opposition areas. The UN states that 76,000 have died in 2014, the deadliest year yet.	Joint defence pact signed by 17 rebel leaders in southern Syria, hoping to attract more backing from Western countries and the Arab states.

2015: The Conflict Deepens

Date	Inside Syria	International Reaction
January	Kurdish forces push ISIS out of Kobani on the Turkish border after four months of fighting. Fighting intensifies around Damascus. The conflict between Hezbollah and Israel in the Golan Heights spills into Lebanon.	Reports emerge that a number of Syrian rebel groups are no longer to receive aid through a covert CIA programme.

Date	Inside Syria	International Reaction
February	The Syrian government agrees to suspend air and artillery strikes on Aleppo as proposed by the UN. However it resumes a new offensive on 17 February, leading to the abandonment of 'freeze zones' on the same day that Staffan de Mistura was to brief UNSC on the proposal in New York. HRW claims Assad is still using barrel bombs despite his denial. Hazm announces it will disband after being defeated by Jabhat al-Nusra in Aleppo. ISIS release a video showing a captured Jordanian pilot being burnt alive.	US and Turkey sign a deal to train and arm Syrian rebels fighting ISIS. Staffan de Mistura announces that any political resolution will have to involve Assad. Staffan de Mistura visits Damascus again.
March	Opposition offensives push back government forces. New Jaish al-Fatah (Army of Conquest) Islamist rebel alliance, backed by Turkey, Saudi Arabia and Qatar, captures Idlib and threatens Latakia, a government stronghold. Southern Front alliance of secular and Islamist groups takes the Jordanian border crossing at Nassib.	The opposition rejects de Mistura's call for ceasefire, saying it would only benefit Assad. The UN and a global alliance of charities including Oxfam and Save the Children name 2014 as the worst year of the conflict yet. The international community is accused of failing the victims and doing little to mitigate the humanitarian disaster. Ban Ki-Moon tells the Arab League he has instructed de Mistura to 'operationalize and flesh out elements in the Geneva communiqué'.

Date	Inside Syria	International Reaction
April	ISIS takes control of Yarmouk Palestinian refugee camp on the outskirts of Damascus, making conditions in the camp even more difficult.	UN announces a series of talks with multiple regional and global parties to assess the possibility of restarting peace talks. De Mistura invites Iran to participate in peace talks despite previous opposition threats to boycott any discussions including the Iranians.
May	US carries out targeted air strikes against ISIS, killing a top ISIS official. ISIS now controls Palmyra, and effectively over 50% of the country. Hezbollah states it sees 'no end' to the civil war.	Low-level peace talks launched in Geneva, meeting with opposition representatives, Arab states, US, Russia and other regional and global stakeholders. Over 30 Syrian opposition groups reject invitation to talks.
June	Kurdish YPG forces seize the border town of Tal Abyad, in Raqqa province, an important link in the supply chain to Raqqa. ISIS kills at least 145 in Kobani, causing 60,000 to flee.	De Mistura criticizes barrel bombs during a three-day visit to Damascus. Geneva talks continue.
August–September	An epic number of desperate refugees spill across the European border, seeking asylum.	
October	Russia steps up its military campaign in Syria. President Vladimir Putin denounces Washington for not being constructive.	

The Syrian Civil War in Numbers

4 years +	The time since the conflict started with the Syrian Day of Rage protests on 15 March 2011.
3 years +	The time since the Red Cross declared the situation to be a civil war.
222,000	The number killed, according to the UN.
55	Current life expectancy in Syria, which has dropped by two decades since the war began.
3.9 million	Refugees who have left Syria.
7.6 million	Internally displaced people who are still living in the country but have abandoned their homes.

Index

A. (fixer), 151–4
Abdullah (boy at refugee
    camp), 35–6
Abidjan (Ivory Coast), 163
Abu Suleiman al-Darani
    Mosque, 76–7, 86–7
Addounia TV channel, 84
Afghanistan, 121, 163
al-Ahmad, Abeer, 85, 104
al-Ahmad, Bassam, 48–9
Ahmed (FSA soldier), 145–6
Ahrar Surya brigade, 128
Akhmatova, Anna, 146
Alawites, 4–5, 13, 15, 53–4, 65–6,
    87, 93–6, 98, 164
  history of, 2, 94–5, 107
Aleppo, 5, 9, 15, 28, 30, 32, 40, 92,
    116, 120–54, 165–6
  Arabic name for, 130
  barrel bombing, 123–5, 132, 176
  destruction of Old City and
    bazaar, 125–6
  ethnic and religious
    diversity, 122–3
  graveyard, 141–4
  history and archaeology, 121,
    123

hospitals, 135–40, 148–9, 172
increase in radicalization, 158–9
named Islamic City of
    Culture, 134
war begins, 89–90, 124–5, 134
Almahatta district (Homs), 114
Annan, Kofi, 9, 126, 164–5
Antakya, 23, 31–2
Antonella (Syrian-American), 41–2
Aramaic language, 37, 39
Armenian genocide, 53
Art House concert, 54–5
al-Assad, Asma, 46–7, 134
al-Assad, Bashar
  and Assad family, 13, 95
  and Darayya massacre, 85, 87
  and political process, 125–6,
    146, 164, 165
  his portrait, 2
  promotes nationalist regime, 98
  seen as winning war, 56
al-Assad, Bassel, 13
al-Assad, Hafez, 2, 12–13, 93–5
al-Assad, Na'saa, 13
Astana, 165–6
Atma refugee camp, 35–6
Azaz, Micheline, 84–5

Bab al-Sebaa district (Homs), 105,
    115–19
  destroyed church, 117–18
Baba Amr district (Homs), 65, 67,
    96, 100–1, 116, 167
Baba, General, 112–4
Baghdad, 168–9
barrel bombs, 88, 123–5, 132, 176
Barzeh district (Damascus), 55, 163
Basra, 95
Beirut, battle of, 109
Belgrade, xiii–xiv, 100
'Believers' (followers of Assad), 5–6
Benghazi, 150
Berlin, battle of, 109
Bosnia, xiii–xvii, 9, 28, 73, 82, 163,
    164, 169, 171
  death toll, 174
Brahimi, Lakhdar, 9, 126, 165
Buck, Joan Juliet, 47
Burt, Alistair, 75
Bustan al-Qasr district
    (Aleppo), 127–9

Carla (Christian in Homs), 117–19
Centre for Humanitarian
    Dialogue, 126
Chechnya, xvii, 109, 163
China, 56, 146
Christians
  in Aleppo, 122–3
  in Damascus, 53–4
  in Homs, 65, 117–18
  in Ma'loula, 37–40, 42–3
Colvin, Marie, 100–1
Congo, 9, 174

Dama Rose Hotel, 3–4, 7–10
Damascus, 1–10, 33, 38, 40, 89, 162–3

car bombs, 10, 37, 43–5
  elite support for Assad, 45–6,
    49–50
  rape in, 21
  two faces of, 48–9
  war begins, 15, 124, 163, 167,
    170–71
Damascus opera house, director
    of, 50–1, 54
Daraa, 14, 36, 176
Darayya, 74–88, 90, 99, 150, 176
Darwish, Mazen, 48
Dayton Agreement, 171
de Mistura, Staffan, 9–10, 125–6,
    165–6, 175
detention law, French, 48
Diab, Mahmoud, 38–9, 42
Dima (actress), 46–8
diseases, return of, 131
Douma district (Damascus), 84, 150
Druze, 49, 94, 164

East Timor, 111–12
Egyptian revolution, xvi, 14, 45, 66

Facebook, 4, 15, 155, 157, 177
Al Fawl, 21
Fisk, Robert, 78–80
Foley, Jim, 120, 151–2, 157–8
'foosball', 139
foreign fighters, 57, 67–8, 87–8
Free Syrian Army, 6, 23, 50, 63,
    66–7, 73, 89, 167
  in Aleppo, 129, 139, 141, 145, 147–8
  and Darayya massacre, 78–9, 83–6
  in Homs Old City, 106–7,
    109–10, 114–15
  in Zabadani, 97–8
'freeze zones', 174–5

Gaza, 62, 113
Geneva Convention, 137
Geneva II talks, 6, 87–8
Great Syrian Revolt, 37

Haitian earthquake, 9, 174
Hama, 13, 15, 36, 47, 92, 124
Handarat bakery, 124
Hersey, John, 100
Hezbollah, 43, 56, 68, 122, 166
Homs, 6, 9, 57, 90–1, 96, 104–19,
    150, 154, 161
  death of Marie Colvin, 100–1
  'ordinary people' in, 114–15,
    167–8
  refugees flee, 40, 164
  refugees return, 115–16
  religious diversity, 65
  starvation in, 8
  war begins, 4, 15, 65–7, 124,
    167–8
Houla, 8, 77, 161, 175
Human Rights Watch, 49, 71n, 83,
    86, 124, 174, 176
Hussein, Saddam, 3, 60–2, 95
Hussein (law student), 64–73, 96,
    106–9

Idlib, 89
Independent, 78–9
informers (awhyny), 81
International Criminal Tribunal
    for the Former Yugoslavia
    (ICTY), 174
International Federation of
    Human Rights, 49
International Rescue Committee
    report, 19–20
Iran, 56

Iraq, 60–2, 95, 163
  advance of Islamic
    State, 169–70
  border with Syria
    erased, 29, 169
ISESCO (Islamic Educational
    Scientific and Cultural
    Organization), 134
Islamic State (ISIS), 5–6, 29, 43–4,
    49, 53, 102, 122, 146
  adopts Raqqa as capital,
    155–6, 176
  advances in Iraq, 169–70
  kidnappings and
    beheadings, 154, 156–8
Israel, 97, 157
  and torture, 62

Jabhat al-Nusra, 6, 122, 154
Jabr, Firis, 57–9
Jadid, Salah, 13
Jawiya Air Force prison, 80
Jews, 6, 113, 123, 157, 170–71
Jibal al-Alawiyin mountains, 95

Kadi Askar bakery, 130, 144–8
Karadzic, Radovan, xiv, 164
Khaled, Dr, 135–40
kidnapping, 22, 29, 43, 102, 151–2,
    154, 156–8
Knissat Bani Az, 21
Knost, Stefan, 126
Kosovo, 9, 28, 163, 174
Kuwait, 6

Lahidji, Karim, 49
Latakia, 12, 15, 22, 93–7, 161
Le Jardin Restaurant, 49
Leningrad, siege of, 51

Liberia, xvii, 163
Libyan revolution, xvi, 14, 45, 66, 113, 154, 163

Ma'loula, 37–43
  nuns in, 37–40, 43
  and support for Assad, 38–41
Makdissi, Jihad, 6
Maria (refugee), 161–2
Matar, Ghaith, 76
Maundrell, Henry, 123
Mezzeh military airport, 83
al-Midan district (Damascus), 55, 163
Milosevic, Slobodan, xiv–xv
Ministry of Information (MOI), 85, 88
Mladic, Ratko, xv–xvi, 164
Mohammed (baker), 147–8
Mohammed (gravedigger), 141–4
Moisin, Sheikh, 142–3
Mood, General Robert, 8, 164
mosques, destruction of, 86–7
Mosul, 29, 53, 95
  falls to ISIS, 169–70
'mouse holes', 105
Muallem, Walid, 88
Mubarak, Hosni, xvi
Mueller, Kayla, 156
Muir, Jim, 165
Mukhabarat (secret police), 3, 90, 102
Muslim Brotherhood, 13, 92

Nada (rape survivor), 11–18, 24–7, 30–2, 34, 36, 64
Narenj Restaurant, 8, 49
Nasrallah, Adnan, 43
'Natashas' (Russian dancers), 4, 7

Negev Desert, 62
Nuremberg Trials, 174

Obama, Barack, 165
OBUA (Offensive Operations in Built Up Areas), 109, 176
olive-oil soap, 134
al-Omari Mosque, 14
Ottoman Empire, 2, 122

Palestinians, 90
Palmyra, 171
passports, 45–6
petrol, price of, 133
Pinheiro, Paulo, 175
polio, 131, 140
prison conditions, 49
Psalm 60, 123
Putin, Vladimir, 4

al-Qaeda, 6, 122
Qardaha, Assad family mausoleum, 12–13, 93–5
Qatar, 6, 56, 97

rakia, 96
rape and sexual violence, 19–24, 27–31, 33–4, 155
  in Muslim culture, 23, 29
Raqqa, 155–6, 176
refugees, xvii, 8, 40, 90–1, 160–2, 164
  Armenian, 169
  return to Homs, 115–16
  and sexual violence, 19, 22, 27, 35
  Yazidi, 168–9
Renda (reporter), 89–91
Rida (businessman), 49–50
Rifaf (soldier), 104–8, 110, 114